Church Folk Going to Hell in a Hand Basket

Beguiled—From the Pulpit, through the Pews, to the Exit

A. Davis
D. Lundy, Ph.D.
M. Maynard, Ph.D.

Poetic Nuggets by C. Wilcox

Truth Serum
Media & Publications

Truth Serum
Media & Publications
Ohio

Unless otherwise indicated all Scripture quotations are from the King James Version of the Holy Bible. Scripture quotations marked (NIV) are from the Holy Bible. New International Version, © 1973, 1978, 1984 by The International Bible Society. Used by permission of Zondervan.
All Rights Reserved.

Truth Serum Media & Publications
P.O. Box 201006
Cleveland, OH 44122 USA
www.tsmpub.com
www.truthserumpublications.com

Church Folk Going To Hell In A Hand Basket
Copyright © 2012 by Truth Serum Media & Publications,
ISBN 978-0-9839280-1-0

Library of Congress Control Number: 2011937105

All rights reserved. No part of this publication may be reproduced, stored in a retrieval system, or transmitted in any form or by any means – electronic, mechanical, photocopy, recording or any other – except for brief quotations in printed reviews, without the prior permission in writing from the publisher.

Printed in the United States of America.

-ACKNOWLEDGMENTS-

Special thanks to everyone at Faith Printing, especially JaNell Lyle for her expertise and guidance, and Laurel Berkel for being such a warm spirit; thanks for your patience and meticulous eye to detail.

Special thanks to Truth Serum Media & Publications Assistant Editor Aliece Stewart and Evangelist Antoinette Clay for their prayers and support.

A. Davis: Wishes to thank God for His countless blessings and favor. I thank my mother, Delores Davis, for all of her nurturing and tough love and my father, the late Marvin Davis, for his wisdom and counsel. I am indebted to my longtime friend Evangelist Ena Davis for all of her support and my Pastor Rickey Wayne Adams Sr. of True Gospel Missionary Baptist Ministries in Painesville, Ohio, for his spiritual guidance. I send expressions of gratitude to all my loving siblings and extended family and friends.

Dr. D. J. Lundy: Wishes to thank God for the opportunity to co-author this book. I am grateful for the careful and constant support of Dr. C. T. Lundy. I am indebted to my daughter Dr. Jennifer for the hours spent reviewing and suggesting important changes. I thank God for the encouragement and technical support of my granddaughter Maia. I send my love to my extended family and friends.

Dr. M. Maynard: Wishes to thank God, my creator, for giving me life and the boldness to believe the impossible is possible. I send a supersized portion of my love to my spouse, children, and grandchild. I send love to all of my extended family and friends.

C. Wilcox: Wishes to thank God, who is the alpha and the omega, the beginning and the end. I want to thank my spouse for being my biggest fan and always supporting me. To my three children who are truly a blessing from God, you are my pride and joy. To my mother, I could not have become who I am without your love and guidance. I send love and gratitude to all of my extended family and friends.

-TABLE OF CONTENTS-

INTRODUCTION...1
1   Flat-Liners..5
2   Disorder—The New Fabric.................................13
3   This Is How We Do It!..23
4   Dollar Dollar Bill Y'all!.......................................31
5   Lest Thou Forget..41
6   Teach and Preach Jesus.......................................49
7   Keep It Simple, Stupid!.......................................55
8   Who Died and Left You Boss?............................61
9   The Hand of the Diligent....................................67
10   Testilying Instead of Testifying..........................73
11   Cool Like That!...77
12   Stinking Thinking..81
13   A Lusting Fungus among Us..............................87
14   Brainwashed and Bamboozled............................95
15   See, Hear, and Speak No Evil...........................101
16   Halfway Saved...107

Poetic Nuggets by C. Wilcox..112

-INTRODUCTION-

Going to hell in a hand basket is an idiom used to identify the hasty downward spiral the church finds itself in without effort. Christendom is out of control and getting worse as the days go by. The bible warns that the time will come when lawlessness will abound in the land. This lawlessness does not exempt church folk. The bible also informs us that God is coming back for a church without spot or wrinkle. This ensures that many things in their current state are getting ready to be shaken out of their places and put back into order. A breaking is coming and it will not be without pain. Here you will find slices of perspective from the authors. Each writer comes from their own experiences and accounts. This book is not about biblical doctrine and is not an educational tour on the bible but about what is transpiring in these end times and where change has to come. The house starts with you. We are vessels, and we should be the walking church. Church is in you and should be everywhere you go.

    The universal church is sliding on a banana peel with one foot stable in an unstable world. Ooh, the taste of a slice of perspective! Satan has not changed his tactics. He is not doing anything differently than he did in the Garden of Eden. The enemy is still beguiling mankind. We are now witnessing the time that even the elect of God are being beguiled. There is no exempt status from the cunning craftiness Satan deals to those who dare to sit at the table and play with his deck of cards. Warning: be careful how you tread when you begin to read this book. The spirit may find some church folk right where they are. I can hear the spiritual Elevator Operator calling out, "Hand basket going down; next stop—Hell!"

We have dared to tread upon the serpent's territory and provided more than the slither he deceives with. We have provided a full slice of perspective. By the end of this book we pray you will have eaten a whole pie.

Now the serpent was more subtil than any beast of the field which the LORD *God had made. And he said unto the woman, Yea, hath God said, Ye shall not eat of every tree of the garden? And the woman said unto the serpent, We may eat of the fruit of the trees of the garden: But of the fruit of the tree which is in the midst of the garden, God hath said, Ye shall not eat of it, neither shall ye touch it, lest ye die. And the serpent said unto the woman, Ye shall not surely die: For God doth know that in the day ye eat thereof, then your eyes shall be opened, and ye shall be as gods, knowing good and evil. And when the woman saw that the tree was good for food, and that it was pleasant to the eyes, and a tree to be desired to make one wise, she took of the fruit thereof, and did eat, and gave also unto her husband with her; and he did eat. And the eyes of them both were opened, and they knew that they were naked; and they sewed fig leaves together, and made themselves aprons. And they heard the voice of the* LORD *God walking in the garden in the cool of the day: and Adam and his wife hid themselves from the presence of the* LORD *God amongst the trees of the garden. And the* LORD *God called unto Adam, and said unto him, Where art thou? And he said, I heard thy voice in the garden, and I was afraid, because I was naked; and I hid myself. And he said, Who told thee that thou wast naked? Hast thou eaten of the tree, whereof I commanded thee that thou shouldest not eat? And the man said, The woman whom thou gavest to be with me, she gave me of the tree, and I did eat. And the* LORD *God said unto the woman, What is this that thou hast done? And the woman said,*

The serpent beguiled me, and I did eat. And the LORD *God said unto the serpent, Because thou hast done this, thou art cursed above all cattle, and above every beast of the field; upon thy belly shalt thou go, and dust shalt thou eat all the days of thy life: And I will put enmity between thee and the woman, and between thy seed and her seed; it shall bruise thy head, and thou shalt bruise his heel.*
Genesis 3:1-15

-Chapter One-

FLAT-LINERS

 Evg. Davis's Reflective Perspective

    I remember in my youth I attended a church that was extremely dead. The deliverance of God's word through the half-hearted pastor was tragically pathetic. We could not even remember what the topic or title of the message was about. The loud moaning and groaning sound he made did no justice to God's sacred word. My family did not waste anymore time on Sunday or any other day to attend this church. A return visit there was usually only for a wedding or funeral. You have to know when you are in a flat-liner's church. A flat-liner simply put is spiritually d-e-a-d. Lifeless.

    I remember on a particular Sunday at this church, things were very chaotic. In the basement, some members were smoking and others were standing around chatting when suddenly we heard above our heads in the sanctuary a big commotion. A literal fight had broken out in the choir stand. The fight was between the pastor's wife and another woman. It was obvious why! After services were dismissed early because of the drama, I saw the pastor sitting in his study with the door opened. He had his shirt off with a sleeveless T-shirt on and a cigar in his mouth. He was talking with another woman about the incident. Giving this scene the benefit of the doubt, it still was not a good look considering what had just occurred.

    What type of impression or impact did the behavior in this church have on anyone? There was a distorted comfort level in the church from the old to the young. It trickled down from the pastor throughout the congregation. The atmosphere was live as you please all week with very little, if any, respect for the house of God on Sunday. The tragic irony is people were deceived into thinking that if they physically and outwardly showed up for service on Sunday morning, this would pay their bill with God. Many church folk still think this way today.

As the years went on scandals surfaced involving this pastor, his staff, and congregants. Sound like with all the news reports in our current day, nothing has changed much with church folk down through the years.

Her priests do violence to my law and profane my holy things; they do not distinguish between the holy and the common; they teach that there is no difference between the unclean and the clean; and they shut their eyes to the keeping of my Sabbaths, so that I am profaned among them.
Ezekiel 22:26 (NIV)

Many of the things we see happening in the church today are not new. The prophets of old encountered the sin of a wicked generation. Ecclesiastes 1:9-10 declares that there is nothing new under the sun. God called the prophet Jeremiah in his day to warn those that were corrupt about doing things their way. Even in those times there were both leaders and people who were comfortable and loved being in their rotten, immoral, and decaying state.

The prophets prophesy falsely, and the priests bear rule by their means; and my people love to have it so: and what will ye do in the end thereof?
Jeremiah 5:31

Yet a loving God, a long suffering God, always seeks to find us and calls us to repentance. In Jeremiah 6:16 God summoned the people to ask for the old paths where the good way is and to walk in it. When we purpose in our heart to strive to be better people and amend our ways, God wants to grant us tremendous blessings. God promises to establish His people in an ungodly world with tangible blessings, safety, posterity, and prosperity. Since God has invested so much in us, shouldn't we repent and give our lives to God in service?

 Dr. Maynard's Panoramic Perspective

It is time for the fivefold ministry gifts to bring the defibrillator out of the back office when they head into the sanctuary. Apostles, pastors, teachers, evangelists and the prophets should be walking under the anointing strapped with a lightweight portable automated defibrillator into services everywhere they go. It is time to send an electric shock through God's people to raise the dead like Lazarus with the unadulterated power of the spoken word. In local churches all across the globe you will find many that are dead as a doornail sitting in the pulpit, dead standing at the podium, dead sitting in the pew, dead shouting in the pew, dead ushers in the back by the exit, and a dead visitor who thought it was a nice service walking out the exit, still dead. You will also find the group that needs to be saved. These are the people on the other side of the exit (the world), dead as expected. It's time for resurrection power to be made manifest!

Flat-liners are people that if hooked up to a hospital monitor, you would see a straight line across the screen. There would be no activity, which would indicate they are dead. The person is dead by cardiac failure or brain trauma. I would like to stress that my use of these very serious conditions are not to make light of them. I am showing from a spiritual aspect the seriousness of such a state in the life of the believer. Anyone called to minister the gospel should know the procedures for emergency first response. The current status of the church is an emergency situation. In first response you are to check, call, and care. You must first access the scene; use discernment to check the pulse of the house. Call God's 911 to release the heavenly host before you put your mouth on it. When God gives you the clearance, prepare to use the AED. Let the Holy Spirit be your guide, attach the pads in the spirit, put the plug in, and push the button. If necessary resume to chest compressions and CPR with the word until the house is revived. It is time for revival to hit so church folk can live and not die.

    An AED is an automated external defibrillator; in the natural a defibrillator does not have the ability to reverse brain death. Brain death is completely irreversible in the natural. It is a loss of all brain function, and the person is clinically and legally deceased. However, the exception is the spiritual defibrillator in Christ, the great I am, the resurrecting power. Christ has the ability to be whatever you need Him to be. It appears some Christians unfortunately received trauma to the brain and have not yet recovered. This means the brain is sleeping.

    It is time for the church to awake out of slumber.

Awake to righteousness, and sin not; for some have not the knowledge of God: I speak this to your shame.
1 Corinthians 15:34

    There are church folk sinning every day. The disgrace of it is that many do not even fully understand the error of their ways. There are some pastors that are not preaching to deliver. They have been preaching a prosperity message to those who are yet bound in their struggles. We have to preach deliverance first to help people understand how to obtain and live prosperously. You cannot put the cart before the horse. Prepare the way like John the Baptist. Help the babes move from milk to meat. It is written in the scriptures that people perish because of lack of knowledge. The leaders are responsible for educating the people. Parents are in leadership roles and are required to educate their children how to walk circumspectly in these end times. We must arise from our slumber while it is yet day. Let the mighty weapons of warfare in God stand up and take their rightful places and preach repentance because hell's territory is expanding by the hour.

Dr. Lundy's Perspective View

The bible often refers to the brain and the heart interchangeably.

For as he thinketh in his heart, so is he. Eat drink saith he to thee; but his heart is not with thee.
Proverb 23:7

Flat-liners are people that come to church looking for their quick fix. As leaders, we must be able to identify these people. They are usually, but not always, emotional hearers. Excitement and feeling good is all that matters. Living for the moment is how they make it through. Flat-liners do not commit because they are not sure what commitment really is. Boredom becomes the barometer that drives them. Expectations are low because they do not believe that anyone really understands them. The fact of the matter is flat-liners are very transparent. They only show up when certain people are speaking or when there is a special program going on. They support select functions of the church financially. There is never any consistency. Their attendance is unstable, and they believe their lack of faithfulness is okay. Flat-liners come for their fix; you will not see them again until the next time they need another one.

I remember the old saints saying, "God is a heart-fixer and a mind-regulator." They prayed for God to keep their minds and to touch their hearts.

Thou wilt keep him in perfect peace, whose mind is stayed on thee: because he trusteth in thee.
Isaiah 26:3

As pastors and leaders, we must remember that it makes no difference what the problem is or what the motivation is, the flat-liner is a person that needs Jesus.

Flat-liners may come into a service empty but should leave fully charged, motivated, and inspired to face another day. Every issue that a person faces in life is mentioned in the word of God. It is up to the pastors and leaders to fast, pray, and seek God's face to have a message for the people. As individuals mature in their walk with the Lord, they will not be tossed to and fro with every wind of doctrine.

So then faith cometh by hearing and hearing by the Word of God.
Romans 10:17

Flat-line churches are full of dead individuals needing to be revived. When a church dies or is dying everyone suffers. As a licensed evangelist, I have had opportunities to run revivals in churches in trouble. Sometimes when you are invited to speak in a church in trouble, you are expected to raise the dead. It is not an easy task to revive a church. You may not have been advised of the situation, but when you arrive you will know there is a problem. It is a cold assembly. The size of the congregation does not matter. Large or small, the signs are there. They could have the best choir in town, yet the church is dead. The pastor may be well educated, and the church is still dead. Seasoned churches are set in their own ways and may try to reject revivals. They think they're okay. The devil has them fooled into thinking that it is not a big deal.

Newly formed churches need to be revived as well because as soon as the novelty wears off, confusion sets in. Assistance is needed to keep the congregation grounded. They must be taught how to operate in faith and not be led by their emotions. Most pastors do not want a real revival to take place because they feel threatened. They take it personally as if they have failed. However, if something is not done as soon as possible it may take longer to turn that church around. If that pastor is led by the Lord, he will start preparing the church for a revival.

Pastors struggle with this because they don't think they need to be revived. The truth of the matter is that after you have ministered to others on a regular basis, you need to be refreshed and restored. Be selective in whom you bring in to revive your church. You can't bring in just anybody. You must ask God for direction. It does not have to be a big-name person, but it must be God's choice. As pastors, we should not look to a friend or someone to whom we owe a favor. Revivals are serious and must not be taken lightly. Get the best person for the job as God leads you. Don't be surprised, but receive the person that God sends.

I received an invitation to speak in a church that I had never spoken in before. I was later informed that as I ministered, the anointing lingered and the heaviness that hovered over the place was lifted for a time. I thank God for using me to bring life to a dead situation. There are many that bring revival to the house, but we need a revival in the land. Let the word of God hit the globe like a tsunami. How do we know if a church is dead? It's not always easy. Sometimes you can't tell by the looks of things.

Having a form of Godliness, but denying the power thereof: from such turn away.
2 Timothy 3:5

Many churches are functioning with a form of godliness with no power. The act or appearance of being religious includes going to church, knowing Christian doctrine and church doctrine, using Christian clichés, and quoting a few familiar scriptures. Flat-liners are caught up in tradition. These religious folks may look better than real Christians on the outside, but the problem is on the inside. They are only acting. People can be great performers. They do not come to church to worship but to perform. Some are position-seekers that love to be seen. Paul warns us about these deceivers. It is our responsibility to make sure the church remains alive with the good news of the gospel of Jesus Christ.

-Chapter Two-

DISORDER—THE NEW FABRIC

 Evg. Davis's Reflective Perspective

I have visited various churches and listened on a regular basis to Christian radio and television broadcasts where the overall feel of the programming was divisive and just pure gossip. Leadership on every level has abandoned God's precepts of order. To try something new is not to forget the foundational structure. I simply cringe whenever I go into services where the word of God is preached out of context. There is nothing but gimmicks and programs available. Many churches are being beguiled by Satan. They believe that in order to reach those that need to hear the gospel, they must compromise. They believe they must change to fit any whimsical feel-good movement that will be entertaining. Sometimes the church house will jump with the choir singing. They may belt out five to ten selections, and then the pastor theatrically serves up ten minutes of half-baked preaching. All of this is under the guise of appeasing and comforting the human nature with God mentioned on our terms. The deception underlies the belief that God will accept any type of worship.

Jesus replied, "Ye are in error because you do not know the Scriptures or the power of God."
Matthew 22:29 (NIV)

The saints want to hear smooth things.

That this is a rebellious people, lying children, children that will not hear the law of the LORD: Which say to the seers, See not; and to the prophets, Prophesy not unto us right things, speak unto us smooth things, prophesy deceits.
Isaiah 30:9-10

The saints are no longer enduring sound doctrine.

For the time will come when they will not endure sound doctrine; but after their own lusts shall they heap to themselves teachers, having itching ears; And they shall turn away their ears from the truth, and shall be turned unto fables.
2 Timothy 4:3-4

Carnality has taken a foothold in the church. It craves something other than service according to God's will. Disorder is having its reign.

My people hath been lost sheep: their shepherds have caused them to go astray, they have turned them away on the mountains: they have gone from mountain to hill, they have forgotten their resting place.
Jeremiah 50:6

We have to bring order back into the house of the Lord!

But if the watchman see the sword come, and blow not the trumpet, and the people be not warned; if the sword come, and take any person from among them, he is taken away in his iniquity; but his blood will I require at the watchman's hand.
Ezekiel 33:6

Disorder—The New Fabric

Intercessors, where are you? The enemy has invaded the camp. Do not come down from your tower. Cry out, pray, and blow the trumpet that God can hear our petitions and heal the land.

Dr. Maynard's Panoramic Perspective

Sister No-way said to her dear friend,
"I like the color gold. I don't know why
they insist on wearing white. I don't know
who that minister of music thinks she is!"
"Gold it is! I already purchased my gold suit,
honey. I don't care what they say; I'll be in it
on Sunday," sister My-way replied.

Everybody wants what they want. There is no longer a reverence in the house of God for leadership or anyone else for that matter. Obedience is a necessity that runs in great shortage in a universal organization that should be full of order. We have become too casual in the church. Pastors have become extremely lenient and some full of compromise to keep people in the pews. Now, instead of churches filled with the spirit, we simply have churches filled with people packed in like cattle by the thousands. The choir sings thirty minutes of various selections, the preacher gives a thirty minute sermon, there is an hour of collection plates going around, and the people go out just as undisciplined and malnourished as when they came in. What does the word of God require of us concerning order? We can start with some r-e-s-p-e-c-t!

15

When church folk are out of order, we get what we currently have: Christendom out of alignment and full of error. It is amazing how much chaos and lack of order can be found in churches across the globe. This is the place where we expect things to be orderly. There is some disorder in the fabric of church today. Preachers are mandated to preach a message of hope and salvation in Christ. There are some preaching from the pulpit reprimanding their leaders and congregants about internal infractions of the congregation. This is what some call "throwing off from the pulpit." The pastor or leader is cloaked in ministerial garb, but in reality they are cougars getting ready to pounce on their unsuspecting foe. They tear into their victims from the pulpit, and only a few know of whom the pastor is speaking. The victim begins to fold up like a cheap suit. There is nowhere to run for cover, and they endure their beating one word at a time. It is a common epidemic and this fabric is a fabric of disorder!

The role of leadership can cause power trips. There are some leaders who, when given a level of authority, change their thinking and actions altogether. They become lean, mean, tongue-lashing machines. These individuals do not know how to talk to people and have poor communication skills. Given a supervisory position, they talk to staff and volunteers as if they are ignorant. I have seen staff and volunteers who are pushed to tears. We then wonder why the work is great but the laborers are few. The pastor is informed of the behavior of these leaders, but because they have close ties with the pastor and give good tithes, these leaders remain in their places.

Dear friends, let us love one another, for love comes from God. Everyone who loves has been born of God and knows God.
1 John 4:7 (NIV)

Disorder—The New Fabric

There are leaders in place that are carrying suitcases full of insecurities. They are afraid of losing their positions when new converts come in motivated to do the things of God. They will pin the converts up like a piñata and use their heads for batting practice until they give up. Many souls have been sent back to the world because of them. This should not be. The church should be a place of embrace and warmth. It should be nurturing and encouraging so that each one will teach one. When I hear the words "law" and "order" I think of the world in which we live. What would the world be like without laws in the land to hold people accountable for their actions? The same applies in the church. We are to reverence God and the sanctuary where we expect Him to dwell and meet us. Instead, we find lewdness, vileness, perverseness, covetousness, lying, and stealing. These are the various shades of "the new fabric" of disorder. There will be church folk busting the doors of hell wide open. Satan's imps (demons) will be preparing a Big Game party. The banner will read "Ain'ts Welcome Home." They will be entering in increments as large as a football field one group at a time.

God does all things in decency and order, and this is the way we are to conduct ourselves. We are to be like Christ in every manner. We must turn and repent while there is yet time. Repentance in the church is a must for restoration. We must get our own houses in order while it is yet day. We are vessels where the Holy Spirit resides. Many seek to justify their actions on their own terms but holiness requires disorder to cease.

Hear the word of the Lord.

Do not be deceived: God cannot be mocked. A man reaps what he sows. Whoever sows to please their flesh, from the flesh will reap destruction; whoever sows to please the Spirit, from the Spirit will reap eternal life.
Galatians 6:7-8 (NIV)

Dr. Lundy's Perspective View

God spoke and by order the universe was established. Nothing can operate cohesively without order. Disorder is confusion. The church should always display and be in order. There are guidelines, rules, and regulations that should be followed. It is important for the regular church service to be consistent, inviting, and uncomplicated. Written programs with the order of the service should be utilized when applicable. There are different types of services that require a change from the routine. The written programs should say, "Subject to change according to the leading of the Holy Spirit." I believe in letting the Holy Spirit have his way. However, I have been in services where everything was out of order and the Holy Spirit was blamed for the confusion. There

Disorder—The New Fabric

is a certain sound and presence that accompanies the moving of the Holy Spirit. There is also a faint sound and eeriness present when disorder has the lead. The latter is distortedly echoing across the globe.

For God is not the author of confusion, but peace, as in all churches of the saints.
James 3:16

    I recall an occasion at a particular church when the visitors inquired why the service did not start as scheduled according to the program. Those that were in charge apologized for the inconvenience and assured the visitors it would not happen again. The visitors decided to give it another try. They showed up the next week only to find the leaders missing in action, and those in charge were not sure how to expedite the service. Apologies were made and they were told that this was not the norm. The visitors returned for a midweek evening service. The prayer started on time but those scheduled to be in charge were not there as usual. There was no backup system in place. The visitors got up to leave in the middle of the service shaking their heads. When they were asked why they were leaving, they let it be known that each time they visited the church, it was out of order. They shared how they just relocated to the area and wanted a place to fellowship because their church was too far away. They also said they would not be returning. This is the fabric of disorder.
    While Moses was on Mount Sinai receiving the tablets inscribed by God with the Ten Commandments, the people convinced Aaron to build them a golden calf. Leaders must be careful, prayerful, and watchful. Aaron wanted to please the people even if it meant sinning against God. Moses was out of sight and out of mind. The people wanted something they could physically see and

touch. People that are not operating in faith are always looking for signs and wonders. They like the "high." When the anointing is not felt in the service, some ministers try to create an atmosphere to stir the emotions. We must set the house in order to avoid operating in a state of apostasy.

Having a form of Godliness but denying the power there of: from such turn away.
2 Timothy 3:5

Christians must organize themselves mentally, physically, and spiritually. There has to be balance in order for us to be productive. Prayer is the key to organizing every phase of our lives. When our lives are chaotic it spills over into the church. When there is an alter call at church and we are asked to bring our burdens to the Lord and leave them there, as much as we try, sometimes when the prayer is over, we pick up our baggage and take it back to our seats. Then at the end of the service we take our baggage back home with us. We wonder why we are still so heavy after a service that was supposed to lift us up. When we as individuals are out of order we are not able to help ourselves or anyone else. This habitual disorder can lead to depression. Depression is one of Satan's chief weapons used to render us immobile.

It is important for us to recognize disorder for what it is and do something about it. Everything done in worship service must be beneficial to the worshiper. Every worshiper should consider their self a contributor. These principles touch every aspect from singing to preaching and the exercise of all spiritual gifts. All contributions to the service must have love as its chief motivation. All participation in worship service is done to strengthen and encourage one another.

Disorder—The New Fabric

When disorder is prevalent in the church we must look at the head. If the head is out of order, the body is going to follow. If you want to know what is going on in the church, look at the pulpit. Some leaders thrive on chaos. Only a few church folk know what is really going on. These people are a part of the inner circle. There are some who have been given the title and responsibility only to find their hands have been tied behind their backs and they are kept in the dark. When tactics such as these are common practices, the unsuspecting members and visitors will suffer. Establishing and running a church is not a roll of the dice. A church cloaked in disorder will never grow. When the leadership is not accountable, what message is being sent to the congregation? A church cloaked in disorder is uncomfortable and hard to endure. God has entrusted the church to win souls. All things must be done with a spirit of excellence. We are mandated to give God our very best!

-Chapter Three-

THIS IS HOW WE DO IT

 Evg. Davis's Reflective Perspective

God allowed my memory to take me back in time. I remembered a church I attended early on in my life. It was a place full of staunch traditions of human effort in the name of God. As you moved toward the entrance of the sanctuary, there was a pious atmosphere and order, like the Pharisees and the Sadducees spoke of in Matthew 15:1-20, which speaks of the leaders of the church that were prominent in the Jewish synagogues.

The Lord says: "These people come near to me with their mouth and honor me with their lips, but their hearts are far from me. Their worship of me is made up only of rules taught by men."
Isaiah 29:13

In examining the above scripture and remembering this church, I now see that we gathered into a physical structure and played church. The spiritual application of the word and the spiritual growth was weak. To what avail or benefit did we apply the word in our everyday lives? The pastor did not preach the word in a way to help us address the problems and situations of our home lives and occupations. This was many years ago and the universal church has grown in its understanding of the word since then. This pastor did a lot of hooping, which is not a good thing when overdone. Hooping is an energetic style of delivering a sermon found in some churches. Maybe, to no fault of his own, he did not know how to help us find God because he was still looking himself. Our human nature intends to do what is right, but when we are taught by the command of humans, who are fallible, weak, and with error, we are doomed to fail and our effort futile.

During these early years of my life I felt the presence of God with me. I asked myself a thought-provoking question: "Why am I here? What is the purpose for the church in my life?" I had a wonderment of this powerful God, but I had yet to seek Him out. I thought that persistent church attendance and following the traditions of the church would fulfill my life. This experience was having an opposite effect on me. I thought all I had to do was be a person of integrity, achieve a career, live a good life, and help people. I had not been taught I had to have a relationship with God one on one. What we were taught at this church was to show up, the pastor knows best, shout, give an offering, and to return the following Sunday. Therefore, it encouraged relaxed, slack behavior and a sense of no-need-to-change. I continued to say, "There is nothing wrong with my life!" I was in a state of denial. As I matured I began to question the many things I saw and began to fervently read the scriptures. The contents of the bible spoke very differently about some of the things going on in the church. I sought God and stayed before Him until He shook loose everything I needed to let go of. I had to let go of the church doctrine that still has so many bound today.

During the late 1950s and the early 1960s, the church had strong moral values, much stronger than they are today. The people were more respectful, easily convicted of wrong acts, and downright shameful in wrong-doings. In those days God was recognized and was reverenced on a national level in spite of the 1960s revolution, which brought about radicalism. The entire nation still took pride in its acknowledgement of "one nation under God." The world has changed its course, and the church has followed. Now, shallowness, worldly hearers, and worldly cares consume us.

Still others, like seed sown among thorns, hear the word; but the worries of this life, the deceitfulness of wealth and the desires for other things come in and choke the word, making it unfruitful.
Mark 4:18-19 (NIV)

 Dr. Maynard's Panoramic Perspective

Son of man, I have made you a watchman for the people of Israel; so hear the word I speak and give them warning from me. When I say to the wicked, You wicked person, you will surely die, and you do not speak out to dissuade them from their ways, that wicked person will die for their sin, and I will hold you accountable for their blood. But if you do warn the wicked person to turn from their ways and they do not do so, they will die for their sin, though you yourself will be saved.
Ezekiel 33:7-9

    I admonish all church folk to consider in depth what they truly believe concerning the word of God. Where is the fear of the Lord in the church? Do the pastors and ministers who preach the word of God believe what they say? On numerous occasions in various congregations, anointed preachers and prophets come into the house of God and administer a spiritual spanking. A word of correction is delivered to the church and the word goes ignored. The Lord sends another messenger in the same churches to reiterate the same theme, but the pastors again refuse to hearken to the voice. The messengers who are invited to minister are not honored by those who invite them. Is this not a chosen vessel? I have been privy to hearing the conversations of leaders after their invited guests have departed. They size up the messenger and dissect everything about them but they do not hearken to the warning. Is the church so perfect that God cannot send correction? I think not; this behavior is detestable! If the leaders will not hearken to the voice of the Lord, then what is the plight of the church?

Saying, Touch not my anointed, and do my prophets no harm.
1 Chronicles 16:22

The reason we do not see or experience change is because change has to be accepted willingly. Tradition and church as usual have made the people not realize what they have become. No one wants to be corrected. This is how they do it. This is how they run their house and they refuse to change. Beguilingly, they have embraced the world's ideology and want fame, notoriety, and financial leverage at any cost. The church has lost sight of what they are put in place to do, though many started out right. The mixture of the church and the world is so intertwined you cannot decipher where either begins or end.

Thus you nullify the word of God by your tradition that you have handed down. And you do many things like that.
Mark 17:3 (NIV)

Mental bondage is never good for the mind of any people. We are now in the year two thousand twelve, and many still believe and hold to the tradition that women should not preach. If God is able to make the rocks cry out if man refuses to praise Him, surely He can use a woman to spread the good news. Women's contributions to the church are often overlooked. The scripture used greatly to push this thought is 1 Corinthians 14:34-35. If we take this scripture literally, then women should not partake in service in any form because to be silent means to not utter a word of any kind in the church. All scripture has to be interpreted in its proper context of all verses surrounding it. This very bible they use to pull this text for a woman to remain silent also identifies Deborah in the Old Testament as a judge and a prophetess. What is a prophet? A mouthpiece for God, are they not? This woman gave council and had greater faith than many of the men in Israel.

This woman of God even was called upon to lead the military. Common sense unfortunately is not always common. Do the very people who hold to this thought declare this one woman was an exception to the rule? Let God use every person who is a willing vessel. Let the church become unified to save this generation who have turned away.

"Tradition is the living faith of the dead; traditionalism is the dead faith of the living."
Jaroslav Pelikan

 Dr. Lundy's Perspective View

Change is good and change is constant. So often, we are stuck in denomination and tradition. We refuse to allow God to make the necessary changes that are so vital for growth. Things that were effective in the past are no longer effective because of various reasons. Times have changed, and the church must also change if it is to remain relevant. God blesses us in our ignorance, but when we come into the knowledge of truth, we must walk in it. Making adjustments and alterations does not mean lowering your standards; it simply means you are trying to obtain a better fit. People are afraid of making changes because they have gotten comfortable. They have pledged their allegiance to a denomination, tradition, and church name instead of putting their confidence in God. Borderline insanity is when you keep doing the same thing the same way and expect different results.

We want so badly to be accepted that even when we know something is wrong, we go along with it. I'm not talking about being rebellious for the sake of being rebellious. I'm talking about being led by the Spirit to bring about a change for the greater good. When the Holy Spirit urges you to speak up against a situation that is killing the church, be ready to do so, understanding the ground has already been prepared to receive it. A lot of guidelines in the church are man-made. God did not have anything to do with them. Fear has caused us to sit back in the church and watch our leaders go down. I know it is not easy to speak up, but at least have an opinion. I always tell my children, "It is a sorry person that has no opinion and is unable to make a decision." I know we do not like to make waves, but do not be the person that says, "I was going to say something, but...." God wants us to know Him and His voice, not just follow religious manmade traditions. The more we know about God, the more we know His voice.

For I desire mercy, and not sacrifice; and the knowledge of God more that burnt offerings.
Hosea 6:6

We must be flexible and open to change if we are serious about going to the next level. God will surround you with people that will be an asset to the church. Suggestions should be encouraged. New, young, and youthful thinkers bring so much to a church. So often we think they have nothing to offer because they have not been though as much as the rest of us. You would be surprised what some of our young people have gone through. A lot of them had to grow up quickly to help take care of their parents and other siblings. Their ability to multitask and spot unnecessary outdated stumbling blocks can be utilized.

When I was a child, I spake as a child, I understood as a child, I thought as a child, but when I became a man I put away childish things.
1 Corinthians 13:11

The church has a problem with change because some people refuse to grow. When we refuse to change, we are saying we refuse to grow up. Change is not an option but a command. It is imperative that we change. Life itself demands change. Some people just want to have their way. It's their way or no way. The Pharisees struggled with the letter of the law. They took pride in knowing the scriptures and having that outward appearance of importance. However, they failed to recognize Jesus as the fulfillment of the scripture. God blesses us in our ignorance, but when we are illuminated by the light, we must walk in it. People still walk in bondage because they refuse to be free.

And ye shall know the truth, and the truth shall make you free. If the Son shall make you free, ye shall be free indeed.
John 8:32, 36

-Chapter Four-

$ DOLLAR DOLLAR BILL Y'ALL! $

Evg. Davis's Reflective Perspective

Today we have pastors in the pulpit substituting emotions for the anointing. Loud preaching does not mean that the spirit of God is on them, let alone in them. Many times it is about extracting financial offerings from the people. After services dismiss, people have discussions. Many are disappointed with the state of the church today. The people are tired of the deceptive tactics, and they have lost faith in the church. Many feel that most preachers are corrupt and find it difficult to join a church. When a pastor or leader is corrupt, there is no way he can truly nurture or feed the congregation. Many pastors refuse to see the error of their ways. They believe in living at the expense of others.

The average sized congregation has limited financial availability, which is a drop in the bucket with the expansion of mega churches. This is why many pastors are striving to go mega. Leaders no longer want to shepherd without an elegant lifestyle. I know of pastors that have been afforded mini-mansions at the expense of the people. To keep with status quo and appearances, they lease limousines; they have them parked in front of their huge landmark church on Sunday mornings. The pastor orders expensive robes for the entire ministerial staff of fifty or more at the expense of the members. Money is collected during fundraiser after fundraiser, and the building still needs its own fundraiser to be repaired.

The pastors and their spouses become accustomed to living elaborate lifestyles. The large amounts of money that pass through their hands purchase their hearts' desires. The sweet daughter rolls up with a classy BMW after another fundraiser. Wow! What a coincidence! You can't get any better than this. Fundraising and conferences seem to be quite lucrative. No wonder there are so many of them going on.

During the offering time, I have observed how the tithe payers are separated from the offering givers. In some churches those with abundant pockets are very highly esteemed and promoted to key positions. Offering times can be a real trip. The deacons create three different lines. They have the twenty dollar, ten dollar and five-or-below lines. All of the twenty dollar givers stand up. If you don't have twenty you cannot stand up. This cannot be a good feeling. What I give to God is between God and me. This is still happening in congregations every Sunday. We must seek God and trust Him to help us rightly divide all things.

 Dr. Maynard's Panoramic Perspective

In the program passed out as you enter the sanctuary, a word from the pastor is inserted. It reads:

"We thank you for the change that jingles but we prefer the bills that fold."
Pastor Money Clip

Money is a necessity for every thriving ministry. Money is a necessity for humanity at large. You cannot obtain relatively anything you need without money except air, and even that is becoming a hot commodity. At gas stations you now pay to get air for your tires. Who would have thought? The world is ever changing and in the times we live, excess and grandeur have become the way for the church. Large flat-screen monitors, cordless microphones, projectors, elaborate furniture—the list is never ending. We want the best of the best and nothing less. I respect wanting what you want, but dig in your pocket and pay for it. It should not be a mandate that the congregants give the pastor the desires of his heart. The scripture says it a bit differently.

Take delight in the LORD, and he will give you the desires of your heart.
Psalms 37:4 (NIV)

Surely the Lord can bless you to save and acquire nice things. He can even bless you with finances from sources unseen. If you have to collect five offerings in a three-hour service, the people are burdened.

But seek first his kingdom and his righteousness, and all these things will be given to you as well.
Matthew 6:33 (NIV)

Greed has grown so thick in the hearts of people that there is never any satisfaction. The bombardment of the requests for money never ceases in many churches. The cunning tactics of those who are trying to get money are always at work. There are times where ministers are invited to speak, and once they have the heart of the people, suddenly and secretly they are told, "We want you to call for the offering now." This is where the minister better beware. The ministers cannot allow the pressure to be placed on them to get the people's money deceitfully. The congregation does not know what has just transpired. The ministers, if not led by the Holy Spirit, will do what the bible warns against; they obey the voice of man. What should be pure becomes tainted. It is hard for me to stomach the auction offerings. The spirit lifts off of the minister and the minister says, "Hundred dollars; who's got a hundred? Fifty dollars; somebody give me fifty. Twenty-five dollars; asking twenty-five twice!" Where in the bible was this kind of ritual performed? When did an auction go downward in dollars? This kind of offering is not of God.

Church leaders cannot continue to pull on the purses and wallets of their members to get what they want when the church cannot afford it. What does a flat-screen monitor do for the congregation when the church only has twelve rows? I'm not against a beautiful sanctuary; that is not what I'm speaking against. I'm addressing pastors that are in lane one trying to drive in lane six without a CDL license. You have to have a CDL license when driving a commercial vehicle and carrying excess weight. Every church is not called to be a mega church! A church with fifty rows or more needs a monitor so the people in row fifty can have a clearer view.

Is it fair that church folk in the congregation are standing in soup lines, while their pastors are eating filet mignon with the guest speakers just paid by the tithes and offerings received? Wouldn't those funds better serve a food pantry to help the congregants and the community? If a pastor wants to eat filet mignon, let him pay for it at his own expense!

And as he taught them, he said, "Is it not written: 'My house will be called a house of prayer for all nations'?

Dollar Dollar Bill Y'all!

But you have made it a den of robbers."
Mark 11:17 (NIV)

Television sure has changed. We have so many networks dedicated to Christian programming now. I thank the Lord for the ability to watch good solid programs that edify the body of Christ. However, I am concerned about the infomercials on gospel program stations. Things are shifting. We are now beginning to view a thirty-minute program that at one time administered the word unleashed with minimal interruptions. Now, you have to pay to hear the word in full. The infomercials for where to purchase the materials take up at least fifteen minutes of a thirty-minute program. This kind of programming is nothing less than money-hungry entertainment.

I have another concern about conferences that have become overly abundant in Christendom. We have many conferences but a lack of change in the world. Who is the church ministering to? Ministries are seeking out the big-name preachers to headline their church conferences. Conferences rake in the dough. Some ministers will not even grace your church's threshold without a hefty fee. The Lord has made their name great and they have been taught they "are worthy of their hire!" We have allowed this to go on for so long and it has gotten so out of control. Even the IRS wants a piece of the action. While God's leaders across the globe sit silently, the government has to open the eyes of the people. I recall hearing a story about a minister that would not even leave his vehicle until he had half of his money up front. Yet there are congregations right now that are struggling financially, scraping together funds to have a great-name preacher come to their church.

Church Folk Going to Hell in a Hand Basket

People will be lovers of themselves, lovers of money, boastful, proud, abusive, disobedient to their parents, ungrateful, unholy, without love, unforgiving, slanderous, without self-control, brutal, not lovers of the good.
2 Timothy 3:2-3 (NIV)

    Pastors and leaders of local churches should be fire baptized, producing the likes of their own kind in the house. They should have good stock in their own buildings. They should stop looking over the fence at the grass that appears to be greener. They will find church folk with gifts right in their own house. They must take the effort to train members of the congregation to be more than benchwarmers. The pastor will discover that trainees in his own house could preach a drunk under the pew. Through the anointing of the Holy Spirit they will have that drunk laid out. The drunk would believe and testify that they had the best drink ever. They would be right, since it would be a drink of the living water. That drunk would never be the same!

    This is my slice of perspective. I'm not against conferences or letting church folk know about the products a ministry has made available to increase the knowledge of the people. God bless you if live an elaborate life because of your own business endeavors. Congregants should be able to see the fruit of their giving. There should be outreach, maintenance of your location and the congregants should be able to also taste some of the fruit from the harvest.

 Dr. Lundy's Perspective View

When I mentioned this chapter title to my granddaughter, she immediately let me know that there was a song with the same title. The song was very different than what I expected. She made me listen to the lyrics and helped me to understand the story that was being told. I came to understand the person the song was referring to. It was someone that started out with such great potential but ended up making poor choices due to pitfalls in her life. She did what she thought necessary to survive. We as leaders must be aware of the times we are living in. It is not about us, but it is about the needs of the people. We must give back, remembering we are here to serve the people in our communities. We must feed the people both naturally and spiritually. With so much devastation all around us, we must fast and pray and seek God's face concerning ways to help those who are in need. We must not go after money solely to fill our own pockets. I am not saying we have to be poor. We need money to function and to do what God has put on our hearts to do. As we obtain wealth through God's grace and favor, let us remember to be a blessing to others.

But they that will be rich fall into temptation and a snare, and into many foolish and hurtful lusts, which drown men in destruction and perdition. For the love of money is the root of all evil. Which while some coveted often, they have erred from the faith, and pierced themselves through with many sorrows.
2 Timothy 6:9-10

When we seek God first, our needs will be met. God gives us the creativity we need to obtain wealth honestly. That wealth is to be used for the furtherance of the ministry. God blesses us abundantly that we may live a comfortable life. We become channels of blessings to others. A pipeline that is designed to carry water from one place to another cannot have water pass through it without it getting wet. It is the same with the people of God. If you allow God to use you to be a channel of blessings, you have to be blessed also.

> *But seek ye first the kingdom of God and his righteousness; and all these things shall be added unto you.*
> *Matthew 6:33*

We are living in a time of suffering and lack due to the poor economy. At one time, people applied for jobs they had a passion for. They took pride in their work no matter what it was. Whether they were a waitress, home attendant, housekeeper, seamstress, executive secretary, nurse, etc., there was a sense of pride in their performance. White-collar, blue-collar, or no-collar, the work was done with honesty and integrity. An honest day's pay for an honest day's work. Everyone worked hard to be the employee of the month. There was pride in receiving the perfect attendance award. Now, people work to get paid. Seniors are suffering because those that are caregivers do not have the patience required for the job. There is no compassion or sensitivity shown to those that are ill. That soothing tone and bedside manner are things of the past. Many people today do not like their jobs, but they need the money.

There are many pastors that have not been called. They want the position for the money they think they will get. They use gimmicks, tricks, and fancy footwork to get money from unsuspecting church members. Rich and poor alike support the church only to find out that when their money is gone, the church they have supported has no use for them. The pastors live in mansions, drive luxury vehicles and wear expensive clothes. Meanwhile, the church goes bankrupt. These leaders are not interested in soul-winning. They are only interested in the next gimmick to get money to line their pockets. It reminds me of Simon the sorcerer who saw the miracles performed by the apostles and wanted to buy the gift of God.

And when Simon saw that through laying on of the apostles hands the Holy Ghost was given, he offered them money. Saying, give me also this power, that on whomever I lay hands, he may receive the Holy Ghost. But Peter said unto him, Thy money perish with thee, because thou hast thought that the gift of God may be purchased with money. Thou hast neither part nor lot in this matter: for thy heart is not right in the sight of God.
Acts 8:18-21

Repent and turn from your wicked ways. Do not let the love of money take you down the wrong path. Money is needed to effectively handle the administrative responsibility of the church, but make sure your heart is right and the money is used and distributed according to the will of God.

-Chapter Five-

LEST THOU FORGET

 Evg. Davis's Reflective Perspective

In these end times, it is a rare find to locate a church that has remained true to God and has not moved from the biblical landmark. As churches start out in the building process, there is a great sense of humility because, at that moment, they forsake not small beginnings. Everyone that is a partaker shows love and respect. Honor is given to the pastor and leadership. The entire congregation is on one accord. However, soon as churches begin to progress materially, amazingly our spiritual equilibrium tends to tilt in the wrong direction. Everyone suddenly forgets the struggle climbed together leaving no member behind. Let us not forget what God has done. We must never lose sight of what is at stake. The only way to remain grounded is through the word being tried in us. When it is thoroughly tried in our lives it is spiritually branded in our hearts. Remember the great things God has done.

God is by our side every second so we are never alone. This Christian journey can sometimes feel lonely. Jesus is a burden-bearer. He has lifted so many heavy burdens down through the years. This is what enables the church to continue on.

Cast thy burden upon the LORD, and he shall sustain thee: he shall never suffer the righteous to be moved.
Psalms 55:22

Consider the universe that is held in place by the hands of a loving God. He has been too good for us to forget where He has brought us from. Church folk can seemingly have short memory spans, and when we are in a crisis we call on God. When things are well we handle things ourselves and forget what the Lord has done. Somebody was pulled off the street, another out of a crack den, another out of the bar; deliverance found us wherever we were. Let us not forget what the Lord has done. It should not take great effort to remember what God has done for us. If you are reading this book, you can read. You are in your right mind and have brain activity. You awoke this morning with no effort of your own. Let's remember the mighty things God has done.

God bought the Israelites out of the land of bondage. They endured slavery for approximately four hundred years. What are the bondages that once held you captive? God is able to keep you from falling. Do not forget what God is doing and has done.

Then beware lest you forget the LORD, who brought you forth out of the land of Egypt, from the house of bondage.
Deuteronomy 6:12

Remember, you have not done anything in your own power. All that you have and all that you shall acquire is by God's mercy and grace. It is the favor that He gives to his beloved.

 Dr. Maynard's Panoramic Perspective

Think of the things God has done for you. There are not enough pages available for me to tell you what He has done for me. I can hear my grandmother Reverend Grant say, "When I think of what God has done for me, my soul cries out, 'Hallelujah.'" This has been the cry of many mothers of the church down through the years. The soul has to cry out because He is the good God! God's blessings are bountiful.

If you fully obey the LORD your God and carefully follow all his commands I give you today, the LORD your God will set you high above all the nations on earth. All these blessings will come on you and accompany you if you obey the LORD your God: You will be blessed in the city and blessed in the country.
Deuteronomy 28:1-3 (NIV)

God says one hundred sixty-three times in the scriptures, "I am the Lord." Make no mistake about who He is. He is the Lord, strong and mighty. He is the great I am, the prince of peace, the wonderful counselor, and the bread of life. There is a song we sing in church that says, "Jesus, I'll never forget what you've done for me and how you set me free." Look over the course of your life and see where He has carried you across desert land. Look and see where He has provided and made a way out of no way.

"I, even I, am the LORD, and apart from me there is no savior. I have revealed and saved and proclaimed I, and not some foreign god among you. You are my witnesses,"

> *declares the* LORD, *"that I am God."*
> *Isaiah 43:11-12*

God has brought many church folk from some dark places. We do not look like where we have been. We cannot afford to forget the things that God has done.

> *Be careful that you do not forget the Lord, who brought you out of Egypt, out of the land of slavery.*
> *Deuteronomy 6:12 (NIV)*

The Lord delivered the Israelites from slavery in Egypt, where their task master was the pharoah. God, by His great power, debunked the demon gods that the Egyptians believed would deliver them. The Lord sent ten plagues against the Egyptians. He first turned the Nile into blood and debunked the god Osiris, the giver of life; the god Khnum, their guardian of the Nile; and the god Hapi, the spirit of the Nile.

During the second plague, God Jehovah made frogs cover the land of Egypt, and He debunked the god Heqt, who the Egyptians believed helped women in childbirth. For the third plague the Lord brought lice throughout the land of Egypt and debunked the gods Geb, their earth god; Isis, the wife of Osiris; and Hathor, the foremost goddess represented by the cow. The Lord debunked several gods in the other six plagues, but the tenth and the last plague was the death of the firstborn of Egypt. This plague was against all false gods, especially Osiris. The Lord, strong and mighty, proved that there is no other god besides Him. Life and death are in His hands. He alone is the creator of everything in heaven and earth. He is the creator of everything above the heavens and beneath the earth. God delivered the Israelites with a strong hand from four hundred years of slavery. This is a great bible study. You can find out more about the plagues of Egypt in Exodus 7-12.

Every opportunity that we get, we should acknowledge such a wonderful savior and all that he has done for us. Christ has saved us from the bondage of eternal death. Let us do what is right and not forget what the Lord has done.

Dr. Lundy's Perspective View

Therefore beware lest thou forget the LORD, which brought thee forth out of the land of Egypt, from the house of bondage.
Deuteronomy 6:12

So often, we forget where we came from. We must always remember to be grateful and thankful for God's grace and mercy. God has been good to us. When everything is going our way, we have a tendency to forget about God. We get caught in the affairs of everyday living, and our schedules do not permit time to pray. We need to slow down and give God all the glory, honor, and praise that are due to Him. When times are bad, in our devastation, we cry unto the Lord. In our heart, we know that He is the only one that can help us. Prior to that point, we exhaust all other options. We think we can handle the situation ourselves. After all, similar situations have come up before and we were able to take care of them with no problem. Sometimes we are even embarrassed to ask God to help us again because we promised God and ourselves that we would not fall prey to the same old thing.

There are times we fast, pray, and seek God's face. Other times we just meditate and wait until we come up with a solution. We seek the advice of others, hoping that in some way they may be able to give us helpful advice. That advice, however, must be something we want to hear or we will not receive it. We follow conferences hoping to get a word of prophecy. We go to great lengths and pay great prices to find answers, but end up worse instead of better. Just as the woman with the issue of blood in Mark's gospel. She suffered with this problem for twelve years before she finally got help. When she knew within herself that if she touched the hem of His garment she would be made whole, she was made whole. Immediately, she received her healing. Her faith made her a candidate for a miracle. Several people touched him and received nothing because they were spectators. They just came to see what was going on. However, this woman had a need that required a miracle, and she got just what she needed.

The children of Israel were miraculously released from bondage in Egypt; however, they soon started to complain about the food God provided for them and everything else. They missed the garlic and meat they used to eat while they were in Egypt. They would rather go back into bondage than walk in freedom. Ultimately, their constant complaining, murmuring, and doubt caused their entire generation to miss going into the Promised Land, flowing with milk and honey. Do not forget what God has delivered you from. Remain humble and grateful. The devil will try to make you think that it is better to stay in bondage and enjoy sin with its familiarity than to walk into your destiny and wonderful promises of God.

Remember who has the hand that can fix your problem. Let your faith kick in, Think of all the times He took care of you. Do not be ashamed to ask the God of our salvation for help, again and again and again. How wonderful it is to reflect on God's grace and mercy. Morning by morning new mercies we see.

For the wages of sin is death; but the gift of God is eternal life through Jesus Christ our Lord.
Romans 6:23

-Chapter Six-

TEACH AND PREACH JESUS

 Evg. Davis's Reflective Perspective

What a wicked time in which we now reside. The very incarnation of Jesus Christ is being challenged on every side. There are even some carnal-minded "Christians" that are starting to challenge the very birth, death, and resurrection of our Lord and Savior Jesus Christ. This in itself is a travesty! The sacrificial lamb was slain for our benefit. There must be leaders that will lead the people to Christ. There must be leaders in the church that will administer the word of God with vigor to an unregenerated world. Every preacher, teacher, leader, and Christian around the world must spread the good news of the gospel. We have to tell the unbeliever about the saving grace of our Lord. Once they have had a taste of the goodness of Jesus, they will never be the same.

Taste and see that the LORD is good;
blessed is the one who takes refuge in him.
Psalm 34:8

Has Jesus truly been preached to you, as Philip preached Jesus to the Eunuch in Acts 8:26-40? We need the word of God to go forth with power to change the state of this world. Who is unable to see the state of America's spirituality? Foreign gods are dictating America's laws and are worshipped in the land. Can we stand to see the possibility of a generation that does not know God? There is work to be done, and it requires die-hard believers! God can draw the people if the leaders will preach the unadulterated word. Preach Jesus!

And I, if I be lifted up from the earth, will draw all men unto me.
John 12:32

 Dr. Maynard's Panoramic Perspective

Jesus answered, "I am the way and the truth and the life. No one comes to the Father except through me."
John 14:6 (NIV)

Archbishop Roy Brown preached "Teach and Preach Jesus" at one of my graduation ceremonies. As simple as it sounds, it was the most profound title any believer could hear. That title has never left my mind or the tablet of my heart. The church does not need more shenanigans and various stratagems. We do not need a whole living room set in the pulpit to comprehend. We need an undiminished word to be edified. We need sound preachers, teachers, and leaders to simply preach and teach Jesus. We need to carry on with the command of Christ himself which says:

Go you therefore, and teach all nations, baptizing them in the name of the Father, and of the Son, and of the Holy Spirit.
Matthew 28:19

Churches desire to be creative and different. The creativity is getting more extravagant and bizarre. When you do the math, what have these creative ideas cost, and does it really make a greater impact? Last I checked, the word of God was powerful enough to form the oceans. It is powerful enough to hold the sun, moon, and stars in their places. The power of God by itself without a PowerPoint presentation cleaned up the dope fiend and took the crack addict off the corner. That same crack addict won many souls to Christ by the testimony of their mouth. Yokes are destroyed because of the anointing. We should be able to preach and teach Jesus without entertaining the flesh. The carnal man enjoys the entertainment and the idea of how far the envelope will be pushed. When a guest speaker comes in with the unadulterated word of God without the slang and the extras, the congregation is bored and is unable to receive. The preacher's job is not to entertain; it is to preach Jesus!

What churches across the globe are in need of is more word and fewer programs. Why do we need a four-hour service when only thirty minutes of it is the word? You may have an additional thirty minutes of praise and worship but the remaining three hours are pure program. It is the word that is going to keep the people. I am not referring to times when God takes over the service. Where can we improve? All of the extra activities are fun but must be in moderation. Fashion shows never led the way to Christ; they lead down the runway. Fish fries never led the way to Christ; they fill a belly but they do not save a soul. Jesus said that if we follow Him, He will make us fishers of men. The only way to effectively change the course of church folk going to hell in a hand basket is to teach and preach Jesus.

Preach Jesus Crucified and Resurrected!

 Dr. Lundy's Perspective View

And I, brethren, when I came to you, came not with excellency of speech or of wisdom, declaring unto you the testimony of God. For I determined not to know anything among you, save Jesus Christ, and him crucified.
1 Corinthians 2:1-2

We must teach and preach the unadulterated truth of the gospel. Our teaching cannot be mingled or diluted with vain imaginations.

So then faith cometh by hearing, and hearing by the word of God.
Romans 10:17

In order for people to operate in faith, they need to be taught the word of God. The bible is our weapon. It is the only language the devil responds to. The devil knows whether or not you have depth in the knowledge of the word. The devil will keep you busy so you do not have time to study. You must find the time to study or you will live a defeated life.

Study to show thyself approved unto God, a workman that needeth not to be ashamed, rightly dividing the word of truth.
2 Timothy 2:15

As leaders, we have an obligation to make sure we give the people the truth. When we accept God's call on our lives, we must take this assignment seriously. We must fast and pray for the Lord's direction. We are to be led by the spirit to give to the people what God has given to us. Sensitivity to the spirit's leading is key to rightly dividing and dispensing the word of truth. Only God knows what message is needed at any given time. By the spirit, He will instruct us on what to say, how to say it, and when to say it.

Your word is a lamp unto my feet, and a light unto my path.
Psalms 119:105

-Chapter Seven-

KEEP IT SIMPLE, STUPID!

 Evg. Davis's Reflective Perspective

In many of our churches, we have become so sophisticated with education. We have more degrees than we can count on our fingers. What I discern in our churches is ego along with that education. The ego is a part of our endemic human nature. I have learned from my own weakness and observed the behavior of others. In order to esteem ourselves, we have a need to impress people with how much knowledge we have. What is happening in the deliverance of this powerful life-changing word of God is we have become imbalanced in the delivery.

The Pharisees and Sadducees during the time of our Lord were the most powerful parties among the Jews. Both in politics and religion they were extremely educated. They were influential groups; some were wealthy and high in position. Their interest in religion was hardly anything more than superficial ritualism. Jesus emphatically warned against false teachers. Study the word of God for yourself. The only way you can spot a counterfeit is to know the genuine truth.

Paul preached the gospel in a simple message to pierce the hearts of all men. This is exactly what God wants us to do.

Preach the word; be instant in season, out of season; reprove, rebuke, exhort with all long suffering and doctrine.
2 Timothy 4:2-3

 Dr. Maynard's Panoramic Perspective

The church is and should be the pillar in every community. Church leaders should be leading the world out of darkness. The carnal influence of the world has no business infiltrating the church. Church folk have a way of making things more complicated than they are. However, common sense is not always common. We are to preach the gospel to all nations but everyone is not called to the nations. Some of us have to be local. There is an old saying: "Monkey see, monkey do." It depicts a monkey that has looked but not investigated. This monkey copied what another had done but had not counted the cost. So, we see many churches wanting to get on prime-time television. Congregations want to be on the big screen. They want you to watch them on a forty-two-inch screen in your living room. Churches are struggling to pay for a thirty minute segment on any broadcasting station. The sad irony is that many cannot afford to pay their water bills or gas bills for their churches. Where is the wisdom in that? Many have elaborate budget plans that are out of their financial zones. If we learn to ride in our lane it would ease unnecessary burdens. Keep it simple!

Satan is looking for as much company as he can to be consumed in the lake of fire. The devil is shrewd, and hell is expanding daily. We have Christians right now who have been saved for a decade and are still smoking. Can this be so? Do you not know your body is the temple of the Holy Spirit? We have Christians that lack self-control and are fighting each other literally in the church. Christian husbands are beating their wives. Believe it or not, Christian wives are also beating their husbands. Love is what should set Christianity apart from everything

Keep It Simple, Stupid!

wayward. Yet there is gossiping, back-biting, lying, stealing, and the list goes on. Do we think we will not be held accountable? Neglecting God's standard of holiness is the beginning of church folk's spiritual demise.

Truth is non-negotiable, and in keeping it simple you have to acquire wisdom. Women with families cannot be at every service. We have to check ourselves. We love the Lord and we want to help. However, it should not be at the expense of neglecting our household and mates. The church is supposed to put women on notice that your first ministry is your home. Parents cannot be so involved in church activities that they fail to know what is going on in the lives of their children.

Picture this: Sister I-got-it has been at church for days. Her house is an absolute wreck with dishes still in the sink. The pastor is hooping a watered-down message and her spiritual condition is the same as it was last month. During the last ten services she has attended this month, she stood in line for every alter call.

Can this serve as an accurate depiction of what is happening with some church folk? We may even be able to say at one time it used to be us. Serving is great, but God wants us to get an understanding. When we get an understanding, then we can keep it simple.

Get wisdom, get understanding: forget it not; neither decline from the words of my mouth. Forsake her not, and she shall preserve thee: love her, and she shall keep thee. Wisdom is the principal thing; therefore get wisdom: and with all thy getting get understanding. Exalt her, and she shall promote thee: she shall bring thee to honour, when thou dost embrace her. She shall give to thine head an ornament of grace: a crown of glory shall she deliver to thee. Hear, O my son, and receive my sayings; and the years of thy life shall be many.
Proverbs 4:5-10

 Dr. Lundy's Perspective View

And the LORD answered me, and said, write the vision and make it plain upon tables, that he may run that readeth it.
Habakkuk 2:2

If you want others to grasp what you are saying, make it plain. Teach with clarity. No one should have to guess what you are saying. Remember, souls are at stake. The truth of the Gospel should not be shrouded with fluff, jargon, or anything that would turn God's word into meaningless talk.

Wisdom is the principle thing, therefore get wisdom; and with all thy getting, get understanding.
Proverbs 4:7

Every leader should ask God for wisdom to lead the people. Remember, they are God's people. We do not know what they need unless God reveals it to us. We should not assume that we know what is necessary to deliver a person. What we see may only be the tip of the iceberg. There may be deep-rooted issues that are not noticeable to the naked eye. When you try to move without the leading of the Lord, that person's condition could be made worse.

Give therefore thy servant an understanding heart to judge thy people, that I may discern between good and bad: for who is able to judge this so great a people.
1 Kings 3:9

Keep It Simple, Stupid!

Directions should be simple, to the point, and easy to follow. God is not the author of confusion. Make sure you say what you mean and mean what you say. One should always be prepared to give an answer to every man. Keep it simple.

But sanctify the Lord God in your hearts and be ready always to give an answer to everyone that asketh you a reason of the hope that is in you with meekness and fear.
1 Peter 3:15

-Chapter Eight-

WHO DIED AND LEFT YOU BOSS?

 Evg. Davis's Reflective Perspective

Time really does pass by quickly. It amazes me how past experiences can still affect you when you think about them. It is almost like reliving the experience. I sit and recollect the times I endured at a church where I committed myself fully for many years. There was an abundance of ministers and elders in that church. Some were already ordained from ministries and churches they had come from. The pastor seemingly had discernment; he was the watchman if you please and a fair man—at least that is what I thought at the time. I remember watching elders, ministers, and laymen vying for positions. One of my friends was already in ministry, and we had similar callings. Although the pastor could discern in the spirit that I had a call, he continually watched me to see what made me tick. He was spiritually sizing me up. He ignored my call and promoted new congregants quicker.

I recall during my years in this church several times when the pastor challenged, degraded, and humiliated me from the pulpit. I could tell when the message was directed toward me. Some of the congregation would look back at me. I always wondered what I had done wrong. I was always ready to apologize and repent if I had offended anyone. He would avoid me altogether, and he continued to humiliate me over the pulpit. I was not a glutton for punishment; I just did not know how to break free. I needed the Lord to release me from this place. The pastor had his favorite ones and he would make it known. I felt singled out and stunned that someone could be so cruel.

My close friend and I were waiting on the day I would be acknowledged and eventually ordained. We awaited the time that I could join her in the ranks so we could work together fervently in the ministry. This church had a lot to offer but only to those that fit in. Ironically, these were spirit-filled, baptized believers. I was stifled in this church for many years, and in the early '90s the spirit of the Lord strongly prompted me to depart from this place never to return again. The spirit of God that was within me was not being respected. I was meek and humble. I may not have had some of the tangible possessions of the world, but what I did have was fire and zeal for the Lord. Leaders are supposed to watch for your souls, which have been purchased by the blood of Jesus Christ. They are like a brain and heart specialist in the surgical unit with your life in their hands, so to speak. They must be cautious with how they use a scalpel or laser. One wrong move and the cut could be disastrous.

The shepherds are senseless and do not inquire of the LORD; so they do not prosper and all their flock is scattered.
Jeremiah 10:21

Dr. Maynard's Panoramic Perspective

Accountability—what is that? Do church folk even know? This is a major area that has been neglected. Accountability has broken down where it concerns the church and church folk. Today, in ministries across the globe you will find all chiefs and no Indians. The respect factor has diminished because we have not been taught to honor one another. Truth states that honor is due to whom honor is due. Pastors do need help; a pastor is only one person responsible for many. This is why pastors select people they believe will be suitable to lead. The problem is that some leaders have been given positions and make calls that exceed their jurisdiction. There is a danger that lies in this disconnected system. Pastors have become so far removed from the people that they are almost untouchable. Leaders no longer report back to the head because the pastors are too busy. How can you ever become too busy to shepherd? Could it be the pastor has acquired too many sheep? Administration does not supersede shepherding, God forbid! To get a meeting with the pastor, you have to put in a request several months in advance. I recall years ago trying to get a meeting with the pastors of a particular ministry. I wanted their guidance on ministerial decisions I had to make. Surely my shepherd should have time to give me guidance; it would only take a few moments of their time. Can a delegated leader make a major call for the pastor?

    In Exodus, Moses' father-in-law, Jethro, shows Moses that he cannot address every issue by himself. He suggests that Moses delegate some tasks to others who are able leaders. These leaders had to be able to rightly divide the word of truth. However, in the delegation, the leaders were to address the simplistic matters but every great matter was to be bought to the attention of Moses. Delegation is the exercise of leadership, not the abandoning of it. Pastors still have to be accessible to the sheep. It costs to be the boss!

But select capable men from all the people men who fear God, trustworthy men who hate dishonest gain and

appoint them as officials over thousands, hundreds, fifties and tens. Have them serve as judges for the people at all times, but have them bring every difficult case to you; the simple cases they can decide themselves. That will make your load lighter, because they will share it with you.
Exodus 18:21-22 (NIV)

 Dr. Lundy's Perspective View

And Miriam and Aaron spoke against Moses because of the Ethiopian woman which he had married: for he had married an Ethiopian woman. And they said, Hath the LORD indeed spoken only to Moses? Hath he not spoken also by us? And the LORD heard it.
Numbers 12 1-2

When you are called of God, you do not have to worry about those that question your authority. You do not have to explain or apologize for your calling. Precious time and energy is wasted on trying to get people to accept you. This time can be spent in prayer and meditation. After you have explained your calling to the best of your ability, they still doubt. Our lives should reflect what God has done to and for us. We are written epistles read by men. People should follow us as we follow Christ. We do not take any credit for ourselves, but we point to Christ. It is because of His redemptive work on the cross that we are walking in this new life.

Moses did not try to defend himself. Moses was a very meek man, and God spoke up for him. We must be careful speaking against God's chosen servants. Miriam was punished and turned into a leper for seven days. Her punishment was limited because Moses prayed and asked God to heal her.

Saying, touch not mine anointed, and do my prophets no harm.
1 Chronicle 16:22

    This scripture is not just talking about pastors. It is referring to all of the anointed people of God. We have to watch what we say about each other. You may not be the in-charge person now, but who knows what the future holds? Be obedient as unto the Lord, not rebellious. Great leaders started out as great followers. God is the one who anoints and appoints.

-Chapter Nine-

THE HAND OF THE DILIGENT

 Evg. Davis's Reflective Perspective

In my lifetime, I have run across "a few good men," which for me refers to people who are diligent for the cause of all mankind. They are men and women that will help others along the way. These are the hands of the diligent. I had the pleasure of running into an old friend at the library, and we reminisced about the past. We talked about when he was a new convert just six months into stabilizing his life in Christ in the early '80s. When he told me about his calling as a pastor, I was completely floored. I remembered how we showed him love and nurtured him at the early stages of his walk with God. Progress is something that the hand of the diligent shows. They are people that continue on the course; things may not happen overnight, but they continue to press. I had the pleasure of visiting the church of this old friend that had been led to lead a congregation. It was refreshing to see the heart of God in this pastor. This is the hand of the diligent.

In the book of Revelation, the church of Philadelphia was able to please God because it was a diligent church. There are many that God is calling for at such a time as this. These chosen vessels are going to be used in the spiritual shift of the church to bring the body of Christ together. The church will no longer be fragmented and full of division. The diligent will always have the supernatural hand of God, not just in the church, but in their home, on the job, and in every aspect of life.

The diligent will still be standing no matter what is happening in the earthly realm. For the saints that remain diligent through endurance, obedience, and uprightness, God has rewards. A diligent church is a treasure. This is the place you want to be. The diligent will obey and hear from the Lord. The diligent church will be of one accord striving in love, being about God's business, and helping one another. When we are submitted to the spirit, the Lord will rest, rule, and abide in the midst of us. A diligent church will usher in and welcome the spirit of God to come in and stay.

Preach the word, be instant in season, and out of season; reprove, rebuke, exhort with all long suffering and doctrine.
2 Timothy 4:2

Dr. Maynard's Panoramic Perspective

Who are the diligent? There are pastors, teachers, apostles, evangelists, leaders, laymen, and Christians in general who are winning souls and are sold out for Christ. They are the diligent! These are the soldiers without veils over their eyes. They are battling the workings of darkness that is beguiling the land. The diligent shall bear rule. The last is getting ready to be first and the first is going to be last. Diligence is intertwined with faithfulness. Every Christian has to have faithfulness to the things of God. They must uphold the truth of the word against all odds. The philosophy of the diligent is to win the lost at all costs. The diligent have a tenacity

The Hand of the Diligent

concerning all things related to kingdom-building. The diligent place no boundaries on what God can do.

For nothing is impossible with God.
Luke 1:37

The bible declares that the sluggard is never filled, but the diligent are made full. The diligent are moving. They understand there is work to do. We cannot win souls looking out of our bedroom windows. You have to be in the workers' circle. Christian workers hand out bible tracks and invite family and guests into the church. You cannot get the blessing by waiting for the pie in the sky to drop for you. Diligence applies to every area of our lives. Go hard for God and you will reap in due season if you faint not.

Dr. Lundy's Perspective View

"That ye be not slothful, but followers of them who through faith and patience inherit the promises."
Hebrews 6:12

Be serious and intentional. Plan to make it. If you fail to plan, you plan to fail. I remind my kids that failure is not an option. Keep getting up. If it does not work, try something else. Do not let go of the reigns. Delayed does not mean denied. Pull on everything you have in you, and then some, to make it. I am not into the sport of boxing, but sometimes I get caught up in the moment. When I see a boxer that seems to be the underdog wobbling back to his corner all bloody in the face, I feel bad and sorry for the person. (I'm thinking he is in the wrong business!) The people in his corner clean him up and tell him to hang in there because he is doing just fine. So, what am I missing here? Can't they see what I'm seeing? There is no way this person can win. Then all of a sudden, out of the blue, this same person gets a second wind and knocks the other person out. This is why you cannot give up. Your next action may be the one to change your situation for the better. If you give up, you will miss your blessing. Remember, we have God on our side, and that is more than enough.

Your walk with the Lord is a lifetime commitment. Be prepared to stick with it. Consistency is the key. We are not walking in our own strength. When you feel overwhelmed, stop and pray. Get your bearings and remember God did not bring you this far to leave you. My father taught me how to drive a car and read a map. He taught me the danger of trying to back up on the highway if I missed my exit. He told me, "There is another road that will get you where you want to go that runs parallel to the one you missed." You can always get off at the next exit and follow the map from that point. There are GPS systems available that make traveling a lot easier. Just as my father directed me, our Heavenly Father directs us.

For in him we live, and move, and have our being; as certain also of our own poets have said, for we are also his offspring.
Acts 17:28

We should study the ant. They never stop toiling. They carry particles much larger than they are. If you stomp their anthill down and pour water on them, they will spring up again. They never give up.

The Hand of the Diligent

Not slothful in business; fervent in spirit; serving the Lord: Rejoicing in hope: patient in tribulation: continuing instant in prayer: Distributing to the necessity of saints given to hospitality. Romans 12:11-13

-Chapter Ten-

TESTILYING INSTEAD OF TESTIFYING

 Evg. Davis's Reflective Perspective

In our churches, we have become accustomed to settling for that which is pseudo, meaning false or a sham. This has to grieve the spirit of God. There is nothing false about a truly awesome God. When we testify, it means giving evidence or bearing witness. In our testimony services we have become nonchalant and make up testimonies just to impress the congregation. When we live carnal lives there is no growth. We all have some type of testimony in the everyday blessings of God. On the other hand, God is waiting to do greater miracles in our lives if we submit ourselves under His authority. God does not want us to settle for mediocrity. He is a powerful God of the extraordinary. When we settle to be ordinary, our lives are bland. Who can tell the greater testimony? A true testimony honors God and is a powerful witness to the people.

 Dr. Maynard's Panoramic Perspective

There are many who have lost the fear and shame of both God and man and will say whatever is necessary to meet their ambitions.
People can make their mouth say anything, and I have heard some whoppers from the pulpit. People are

easily deceived because they believe what the leaders say hook, line, and sinker. Like the church of Ephesus, many false apostles abound. They abandon their assigned duties and do not feed the sheep. They have lost their first love; the sheep are now harkening to the voice of strangers. Today's church is yielding like the church in Pergamum to the persecution and apostasy. It's full of compromisers and pretenders with their own agendas robbing both the borrowers and the lenders. The persecution and apostasy is from within.

False doctrine has found its way into the building. Christianity has blended with the false religions of the world. Like Thyatira, we see church folk have lost their way under the guidance of a Jezebel spirit. They are scattered and led by false prophets. Like Sardis, they are sleeping, believing that they are alive but are dead. Like the five virgins, they are unprepared for the bridegroom. The church's sin will not go unpunished. Like Laodicea, they shall be judged. They believe they are righteous and are in danger of losing their souls. Church folk better fall on their faces like the church of Philadelphia, the loving church with the open door. They had no rebukes. They kept God's word and refused to deny His name though they were weak. Smyrna had no rebukes and was full of the martyrs. Where are the martyrs of this day who are ready to die for Christ? Who will awake from the slumber of death only to find themselves in the bowels of hell? Where are we today, Christendom? Repent while there is yet time!

> *Go up and down the streets of Jerusalem, look around and consider, search through her squares. If you can find but one person who deals honestly and seeks the truth, I will forgive this city. Although they say, 'As surely as the* LORD *lives,' still they are swearing falsely."* LORD, *do not your eyes look for truth? You struck them, but they felt no*

Testilying Instead of Testifying

pain; you crushed them, but they refused correction. They made their faces harder than stone and refused to repent'
Jeremiah 5:1-3 (NIV)

Dr. Lundy's Perspective View

By faith Enoch was translated that he should not see death; and was not found, because God had translated him: for before his translation he had this testimony, that he pleased God.
Hebrews 11:5

What is your testimony? Learn to testify according to where you are. You do not have to make up anything or exaggerate. Your testimony is what God has done for you, nothing more and nothing less. Keep it personal and about you. You cannot testify for someone else. The facts are all you need to tell of God's goodness. Do not tell all of your private business in public. There are some things you can share in an open testimony service, while other things are better said privately in your prayer closet.

75

-Chapter Eleven-

COOL LIKE THAT!

 Evg. Davis's Reflective Perspective

Over the years I have seen the atmosphere change in our churches. It seems the more prosperous we become, the greater our egos rise. There is nothing wrong with prosperity as long as we honor God. Our human nature judges a book by its cover without reading the contents. When we take our eyes and mind off of God and place a human being where God should be, we are in trouble. This has to grieve the core of God in worshipping the created creature more than the creator. Worship belongs to God. There is a difference between worship and honor. We had better get a grip on what carnality is and does. The bible states that to be carnal-minded is death and enmity against God. It is one thing to admire the accomplishments of others but another thing when we start worshipping any person within the church.

Have we given pastors undue authority over common affairs that God can give us guidance on? I know of someone who was so entranced by her pastor, she lost a sense of herself. She, along with many others, did not realize they were worshipping the creature over the creator. During a phone conversation, she stated the Lord was prompting her to go back to college and get an education. She told me she would pray about it and ask her pastor. I asked what the outcome was several days later, and she said the pastor told her not to go back to school. I pondered this and wondered why would this not be a good thing? Is this the type of influence this pastor was given, and no one should think to question his counsel? She came to the point where she could no longer distinguish God's voice from the pastor's voice.

In this particular congregation there was a sense of loving the limelight. This type of mindset takes away from the presence of God. We are consumed with personality and not God. Some leaders are so smooth, they have preached congregants out of their life savings. If we do not learn how to try the spirits we will be swept away and not realize it until we arrive on the other side of the road.

Dr. Maynard's Panoramic Perspective

Church folk with swagger, say what? We have church folk that have acquired celebrity status in the church. The next reality show to come is *Preaching Amongst the Stars*. The term "swagger" can mean a variety of things; it could pertain to having a certain aura. Having swagger indicates a person has real pizzazz; they are stunning and attractive to the eyes. Church folk with swagger look like wealth, they talk like wealth, and they live like wealth. It also means they are trend-setters and brand-builders. Is this what Christ wants us to be? Those with swagger can speak the language of the times and know the lingo quite well. The definition of swagger as defined in Miriam-Webster dictionary is a bit different. It reads: "To conduct oneself in an arrogant or superciliously pompous manner; especially: to walk with an air of overbearing confidence." It is church folk gone wild. The shenanigans never seem to stop. Church folk's main goal should be to win souls to Christ. Let that be your brand.

When church folk enter a building, demons should start cowering in corners. The presence of God should be so heavy on the ministers and leaders, like the days of Moses. The people should see the glows on their faces knowing they have been before their maker. It is time to be so in tune with God that His presence is undeniably manifested in sanctuaries at every service. The shackles should be falling clean off every sinner that comes in the building. It is time for this generation to proclaim the word of God fearlessly and with boldness. Prosperity messages must teach more than material possessions and outward appearances. The people need to be taught to reverence and fear God; this is the beginning of wisdom.

What good will it be for a man if he gains the whole world, yet forfeits his soul? Or what can a man give in exchange for his soul?
Matthew 16:26 (NIV)

Dr. Lundy's Perspective View

Be careful of your conversation with the devil. He knows the scripture. He deliberately changes the word to see if you know the scripture. He is consistently challenging you to make you say something God has not said. In Eve's attempt to correct what the devil said, she changed what God said.

And the LORD God commanded the man, saying, of every tree of the Garden thou mayest freely eat. But

of the tree of the knowledge of good and evil, thou shalt not eat of it: for in the day that thou eatest thereof thou shalt surely die.
Genesis 2:16-17

Life's circumstances will afford times when we are vulnerable. It is during these times the devil will try to take advantage of us. Satan pays close attention to what we say and how we respond. Satan cannot read our minds but does try to plant negative thoughts for us to act upon. Many negative acts are derived from doing what we want and then blaming our actions on the devil.

Let no man say when he is tempted, I am tempted of God: for God cannot be tempted with evil, neither tempteth he any man: But every man is tempted, when he is drawn away of his own lust, and enticed. Then when lust hath conceived, it bringeth forth sin and sin, when it is; finished, bringeth forth death.
James 1:13-15

People should always see Christ in us. As leaders, we cannot be "smooth operators" in the sense that we want people to look at us and not at Christ. We should not use our influence to lead people along and cause them to walk in confusion. The scripture should not be taken out of context to suit our agendas. Do not twist God's word for your personal gain. We have been placed in leadership roles to help lead and guide in all truth.

-Chapter Twelve-

STINKING THINKING

 Evg. Davis's Reflective Perspective

I witnessed the life my dear friend lived before me thirty-one years at a particular church. Her love for her pastor was strong even until her death. She did not waiver in her loyalty to him, his staff, or the church even though she had taken overbearing abuse. They wanted to keep her on a level that did not surpass their own. The only way they assisted her was in ways that she remained subordinate to them. She was a pure and sweet person, and they took advantage of her love and kindness. There comes a time when you have to stand firm in the truth. This can be done without disrespect as long as the spirit of the Lord guides us.

I strongly believe my friend's shepherd was intimidated by her pureness, humility, tenacity, and love for God. She had a strong prophetic anointing. I believe the pastor was afraid of her stealing his thunder. I know there is order in God's kingdom, and she followed protocol to the max. Anytime she had ideas or projects she wanted to bring forth, she always presented it to her pastor. If he did not show he thought much of it, she would scrap it. Some leaders make you feel bad if you create projects that they did not come up with themselves. The pastor told his congregants that he was the only prophet in his church and no one else will prophesy over his authority.

Pride and arrogance is dangerous. Pride comes before destruction, and those that walk in pride God is able to abase. Pride is an abomination to God, and He resists the proud. Some leaders want to look good at all costs, and they will fleece the flock to accomplish it. Before my friend passed, she explained to me the abuse her pastor had suffered as a child. She felt that was to blame for his behavior. However, I believe when God calls us to leadership positions, we must get healed of past emotional abuse, bitterness, wrath, anger, unforgiveness, and negative feelings. This does not come overnight, but is a process. We had better strive to do so. In ministering to others we can cause major setbacks and outright spiritual damage, especially to vulnerable people. I can assure you God will require blood on our hands if we deliberately damage His people He purchased with His blood. He paid a very high price!

If we think we can build on other people's talents and take the credit, it speaks very loudly that we ourselves are insecure. The favor and anointing will not stay very long. When God gives talents and gifts, it is because he wants to use them for his purpose, not our own. If we choose to stay in a church or ministry where we are not honored and ignore the voice of God to depart, this will not only diminish our anointing and productivity, but we will eventually wither on the vine.

Then he told this parable: "A man had a fig tree growing in his vineyard, and he went to look for fruit on it but did not find any. So he said to the man who took care of the vineyard, 'For three years now I've been coming to look for fruit on this fig tree and haven't found any. Cut it down! Why should it use up the soil?'"
Luke 13:6-7 (NIV)

 Dr. Maynard's Panoramic Perspective

Whoever came up with the saying, "Every man for himself and God for us all," must have been thinking about how church folk behave. Many Christians are afraid to help others unless they reap benefits also. The question the one in power asks is, "What does this do for me?" It is almost like climbing a corporate ladder, but instead there is a steeple. There stands a flesh-eating monster on every level, and if you are weak you will be devoured. Many Christians, including leaders, do not want to assist in anything. Most are scared you will be promoted. There are those who want to assist you in everything that you do so they can say they made you. Then we have those who are more common; they want to be made on the back of your talents without acknowledging you. Church folk are not to be so contrary. This is the worldly thinking. Church folk should be godly people that operate in the fruits of the spirit.

But the fruit of the Spirit is love, joy, peace, forbearance, kindness, goodness, faithfulness, gentleness and self-control. Against such things there is no law.
Galatians 5:22-23 (NIV)

The fruits of the spirit should be the aura of believers. Every Christian should always show love; it should not be conditional. It should be what we possess in full volume because God is love. In Christ we should always have joy. It should be the joy that is unspeakable, meaning hard to define yet it's down to the core of your bone marrow. We should be able to tell people about this peace that we have obtained. It's an inner core peace unbelievable to the unregenerate soul. We should have a peace that guards us even in the midst of darkness. We do not have to fear because this peace says God is with us. Can we find church folk today that can talk to the world and illuminate a room with these very attributes? We should have forbearance, which is simply keeping calm in a provoked situation. All Christians should have a certain level of self-restraint.

    We should be overflowing in kindness. It is an action that is shown even when many do not reciprocate the same. God wants us to show goodness because we are made in his image and his reflection is goodness unleashed upon an undeserving humanity. Faithfulness is a must in the life of a believer. We should always be reliable and dependable. Gentleness is a necessity when there is the need for a tender touch or a tender word in delicate situations. The last is self-control, and this one seems to be the one that many church folk are struggling with. Nevertheless, every person is accountable for the choices that we make. Many of these attributes go hand in hand when trying to define them, but they are all needed and we should possess them all in purest quality and in great quantity.

Dr. Lundy's Perspective View

The thoughts of the righteous are right: but the counsels of the wicked are deceit.
Proverbs 12:5

    There are instances when it seems difficult to remain positive. The responsibility of daily living can weigh heavily on anyone. It is at these moments we have

Stinking Thinking

to remember where our help comes from: God. When you are down and out, remember that God has not forgotten about you. You may be tempted to share your feelings with friends, but be very careful when sharing your personal feelings with others. All those that you think are friends may just be there for the ride and hoping that you fail.

Stinking-thinking blood-sucking leeches will drain you. Do not be deceived. You must pray about people you allow in your space. God will give discernment concerning the intent of those that are around you. Pay close attention to the little details that are revealed, both good and bad. Know who the positive people are in your life. It is a true saying that no man is an island and no man stands alone. It is good to have a prayer group or someone that can agree with you on a positive level.

Again I say unto you, that if two of you shall agree on earth as touching anything that they shall ask, it shall be done for them of my Father which is in heaven. For where two or three are gathered together in my name, there am I in the midst of them.
Matthew 18:19-20

Guard everything God has given you. Guard your heart, your gift, your ministry, and your vision from snipers and terrorists that will try to abort your baby. Stay true to your vision by avoiding toxic relationships. They may start out as harmless friendly encounters. The change may be subtle at first, but you will begin to recognize when that relationship is no longer a healthy one. Pay attention to your instincts. Take your hand out of the lion's mouth slowly. Leave your coat if you have to, as Joseph did. God will separate you from people that you may not have the strength to cut off yourself. When He delivers you from people, stay delivered. Some people are in your life for a reason and a season. You have to be willing to allow God to direct you to those that will add and not take away.

-Chapter Thirteen-

A LUSTING FUNGUS AMONG US

Evg. Davis's Reflective Perspective

The spirit of the Lord will not allow me to be passive on this issue. It is destroying lives, families, churches, and society. We can no longer put our heads in the sand. What is happening in the world is affecting the church as well. It is sad to see church folk taking their cues from the world instead of God. Lack of leadership, discipline, commitment, a true relationship with God, and most of all prayer are contributing factors. I have witnessed over the years more women than men in attendance at church. This has caused an imbalance. Pastors and leaders are succumbing to the fierce temptations. Either they are seducing or being seduced. If the pastor fears God, there is a greater chance that his congregation will line up. If there is a problem, the pastor will move quickly to nip it in the bud. Most importantly, the pastor's life has to line up with the scriptures. God knows we have weaknesses, but we must make an effort to come to Him for help.

Confess your faults one to another, and pray one for another, that ye may be healed. The effectual fervent prayer of a righteous man availeth much.
James 5:16

The church is and should be a refuge. Its core existence is in place to win souls and teach the faith until Jesus Christ's return. The church stresses the importance of purity and marriage. Church folk are allowing sexual sins to take a stronghold, and it is tearing some churches apart. God's word speaks strongly about sexual sins. Worldly influences have caused people to believe if they fear and obey God and abstain from unwed sexual relations, they will be ostracized. This has become a major attack on our young people.

Put to death, therefore, whatever belongs to your earthly nature: sexual immorality, impurity, lust, evil desires and greed, which is idolatry.
Colossians 3:5 (NIV)

 Dr. Maynard's Panoramic Perspective

People do not want to be preached at; they want to be preached to. I have heard this said many ways. I agree they want to be preached to about wealth, success, increased possessions, and new husbands and wives. They don't want to be preached at because then you are speaking to them directly and the spirit is uncovering their sin. They prefer to hear what justifies them remaining in their error. They came to church to hear a feel-good message, not to get their house in order.

I see more unwed pregnancies in the church than I do at the prenatal department in the hospital. Many of these faces have been in the church house a long time. What didn't they hear in the messages? How come conviction didn't meet them in the bedroom? Where are we failing to change the mindset? The television is telling our younger generation that this is normal. Through televised scripts, a message is being conveyed that unwed sexual relationships are not bad. Our young people are buying the lie that there is no penalty, just pleasure that awaits them. We cannot just preach about the promises of God without helping the people understand the penalties of sexual immorality.

Church folk are making spectacles of themselves before the world. Pastors' wives are in local news media fighting in the sanctuary. Deacons are fighting with blows of fury. I was watching the local news one night, and they showed a deaconess slap a deacon and he punched her out! We have entered a time of the great unveiling. Church pastors, leaders, and teachers are being revealed and uncovered. They are being exposed as pedophiles. We are seeing a vast array of perversions and sexual misconduct that is shocking to the conscience. Sexual immorality is increasing on every side. Sensuous church folk divas are showing cleavage, and their dresses are hugging hips. They have big Botox-shot lips and colored finger tips.

> *With her much fair speech she caused him to yield, with the flattering of her lips she forced him. He goeth after her straightway, as an ox goeth to the slaughter, or as a fool to the correction of the stocks; Till a dart strike through his liver; as a bird hasteth to the snare, and knoweth not that it is for his life. Hearken unto me now therefore, O ye children, and attend to the words of my mouth. Let not thine heart decline to her ways, go not astray in her paths. For she hath cast down many wounded: yea, many strong men have been slain by her. Her house is the way to hell, going down to the chambers of death.*
> *Proverbs 7:21-27*

Church folk are viewing pornography or watching it together. I remember early on in my studies, there was a minister who taught in a class that what you do in your bedroom with your spouse is an "anything goes" party. We were told that once you are married, the bed is undefiled. So, I leave you to answer this question: Would it sit well for a Christian couple to view pornography of sinners in all acts of lewdness? Is that appropriate entertainment? I cast down every vain imagination that would rise up against God! New ideas of what is alright keep emerging because people are looking to satisfy their own vile lusts. What do sinners in sexual acts do for a Christian marriage? It will bring some fire to your marriage alright. You better read what happened to Aaron's sons when a strange fire entered in!

Aaron's sons Nadab and Abihu took their censers, put fire in them and added incense; and they offered unauthorized fire before the LORD, contrary to his command. So fire came out from the presence of the LORD and consumed them, and they died before the LORD.
Leviticus 10:1-2 (NIV)

Leaders and congregants alike are leaving their spouses for other lovers. The lover is in the same exact church house. I have literally seen leaders dump their spouse and remarry someone else in the congregation, and everybody stayed in the same church. Now, that is no shame for you! Lust is like a fungus; it continues to grow if left untreated. The universal church has been silent for so long that the fungus has spread like a wildfire, and now there is a need to call in the National Guard Firefighters. How can the world believe and trust church folk who are as corrupt as the world? Hell gates are waiting to consume their flesh by fire. We must teach the necessity of repentance!

A Lusting Fungus among Us

But mark this: There will be terrible times in the last days. People will be lovers of themselves, lovers of money, boastful, proud, abusive, disobedient to their parents, ungrateful, unholy, without love, unforgiving, slanderous, without self-control, brutal, not lovers of the good, treacherous, rash, conceited, lovers of pleasure rather than lovers of God— having a form of godliness but denying its power. Have nothing to do with such people.
2 Timothy 3:1-5 (NIV)

Dr. Lundy's Perspective View

And the Scribes and Pharisees brought unto him a woman taken in adultery, and when they had set her in the midst they say unto him, Master, this woman was taken in adultery, in the very act. Now Moses in the law commanded us that such should be stoned, but what sayest thou?
John 8:3-5

There have always been double standards as far back as I can remember. Women were supposed to keep themselves chaste and pure, and I agree with that. The men were taught to prove their manhood by deflowering as many females as possible before getting married. Down through the years, mothers have talked to their daughters about keeping themselves until they get married. The church has been teaching young women Christian ethics for years. However, we are hard-pressed to find Christian counseling for men concerning these issues. Most churches do not have, nor do they feel the need to offer, this type of counseling. We teach that it is important for a female to be a virgin until she is married, but young men are laughed at if they are.

We have all asked the question pertaining to the women caught in the very act of adultery. Where was the man? It takes two to tango, as they say. You must set a standard for yourself. Do not allow society to dictate your personal sex life. Even though so many have contracted incurable diseases, society leads you to believe it is all harmless. If someone is truly interested in you they should be willing to wait. This is why the scripture tells us not to be unequally yoked. If you are a Christian dating another Christian, you both have the same core values and know what is at stake.

Whoso findeth a wife findeth a good thing, and obtaineth favor of the Lord.
Proverbs 18:22

God designed the body. He knows our needs and desires. Have faith and trust God to send your exact match. Some people get married while others remain single all their lives. All of that is between the individual and God. At times, we try to play matchmaker for our friends and family. We make single people feel guilty or incomplete if they are not married by a certain age. Some have even gone as far as to think something is wrong with them mentally or physically. Society has led us to believe the only way to be happy is to have the perfect shape, weight, height, and color according to their standards. Happiness according to the powers that be means having a spouse, two kids (one boy and one girl), a home with a white-picket fence, a two-car garage, and a chicken in every pot. We are out of control trying to please others. We must learn to trust God by faith and allow His grace and mercy to carry us through. Paul addressed some of these issues with the Corinthians.

For I would that all men were even as I myself. But every man hath his proper gift of God, one after this manner and another after that. I say therefore to the unmarried and widows, It is good for them if they abide even as I. But if they cannot contain, let them marry: for it is better to marry then to burn.
1 Corinthians 7:7-9

-Chapter Fourteen-

BRAINWASHED AND BAMBOOZLED

 Evg. Davis's Reflective Perspective

In the '70s I attended a church that would change my life forever. I was very impressionable and wanted to please God no matter what. Some of the traditions and rules of the church became branded and deeply rooted in my mind. I was to the point of being borderline brainwashed. To the pastor's credit, he was instrumental in my Christian conversion. He was very gifted and full of energy and he utilized all of us. The problem was that we spent more time in church than we did at our own homes. It was exciting in the beginning because it was a time of spiritual self-discovery. Our pastor knew he had our full commitment. Starting so fresh and so young, our love for God was pure and innocent. In our eagerness to serve we were taken advantage of because of our young spirituality.

The word of God suddenly began to become manipulated and misconstrued. It became an entrenched belief that if we disobeyed the leadership in any way, we would surely be facing "hell, fire, and brimstone." We began to believe our whole lives were centered on this church. We spent all of our vacation time going to their conventions, even though we had families of our own. The church folk took advantage and manipulated my friendship, kindness, and vulnerability. The time came when I was in great need. I could count on one hand the people in the church that helped me. I recall the pastor telling me we are to help our brothers and sisters in the Lord. He said we should assist with whatever substance and resources we have. I still ask the question, where were they when I had a major need? I was fleeced until there was no more in the bank account. I paid my tithes and offerings faithfully and was committed to service. Only my family showed up on the scene to help me pick up the pieces.

This experience did not sit well with my family. To this very day they are skeptical about churches. All my giving of time and resources in this church became futile in a natural sense. I know with God, my giving is never in vain. I began to move from location to location after that, without finding stability for a long time. Churches today are lacking stability for their congregation. They should be a second home and a safe haven.

What you do in the dark will be brought to the light. When you discover a leader is not who you thought they were, it can leave emotional scars that can take years to heal. You must keep your eye on Jesus. This will save you a lot of heartaches and pain. The bible says, "Man will fail you." My family thought I was brainwashed and taken advantage of on so many levels. When I look back on my life I can see that I was. Innocently, I put faith in a shepherd. Shouldn't the sheep be able to trust the shepherd to care for their souls? I was consumed with pleasing my pastor and the church; I was brainwashed and bamboozled.

Then I will give you shepherds after my own heart, who will lead you with knowledge and understanding.
Jeremiah 3:15

 Dr. Maynard's Panoramic Perspective

I had the opportunity to see some of the good old boys get together and throw their weight around. The good old boys are some of the male leaders of the church. These male leaders believed women should remain in the kitchen. I recall signing up for a class at a particular church. I was registered, but on the day classes were to begin I was met in the lobby by a leader. I was informed I could not take the homiletics class at their church. I was told this class is reserved for men only and they do not believe that women should preach. I already possessed a doctorate degree and had proven such with school records. I had taken homiletics before during college; I just wanted a refresher course and another view on the subject. Anyone that knows me will tell you I love a classroom. I was in such disbelief. I was told I could take any other class that they had available? I said, "No, thank you," and kicked the dirt behind me as I walked away. I could not believe it. That had to be a joke, right? Women are still trapped under this kind of teaching today. They are brainwashed into believing God cannot use them for anything more than getting the good old boys a meal and a cup of coffee.

The word of the LORD came to me, saying, "Before I formed you in the womb I knew you, before you were born I set you apart; I appointed you as a prophet to the nations."
Jeremiah 1:4-5

 Dr. Lundy's Perspective View

And the LORD God said unto the woman, what is this that thou hast done? And the woman said, the serpent beguiled me, and I did eat.
Genesis 3:13

When I think of the words "brainwashed" and "bamboozled," two people come to mind without hesitation. The first is Jim Jones, who deceived the people into taking poison. There were 909 that committed suicide. They were brainwashed into believing their decision would lead them into glory with God. The second is Adolf Hitler; he used his influence to order the execution of eleven million people and was driven by pure hatred. Of course, there are many others that have wreaked havoc and terror in this world. In our quest to find blissful existence, we allow the devil to show us mirages. He leads us to believe that we have found an oasis in the midst of the desert, but it does not exist.

There are some people that like to control others. There are some people that like to be controlled. When evil motivation is the guiding factor, the results are devastating to both parties. If you are an influential person, you must influence positively for the good of all involved. If you allow others to control you, you are yet responsible for your actions. There are sins of commission and omission. Do not blame others for making decisions for you. You have a choice in the matter and you will be held accountable. We must learn to speak up for what is right and speak against what is wrong. We should not take advantage of each other. If you are in leadership, remember that God has placed you there as a servant to do the right thing. Others are depending on you and trust you to be fair and just. A leader has to remain prayerful. We cannot be careless with the things of God. There is no room for deception and leading others into a false sense of security.

Let the words of my mouth, and the mediation of my heart be acceptable in the sight, O LORD my strength, and my redeemer.
Psalms 19:14

-Chapter Fifteen-

SEE, HEAR, AND SPEAK NO EVIL

 Evg. Davis's Reflective Perspective

In many churches we can find carnality thicker than a slice of country ham. Carnality has crept in to the point where pastors have omitted more important matters and nitpick over trivial matters. Anytime there is favoritism being shown in the church and is prevalent, it is due to carnality. Many pastors are aware that serious sins are being committed by their popular and favored congregants, yet these sins are covered and swept under the carpet. The pastor is supposed to give correction. God forbid if we are not among one of the favored. These are the sins that are under microscopic investigation and practically and indirectly announced over the pulpit through the messages.

For there is no respect of persons with God. For as many as have sinned without law shall also perish without law: and as many as have sinned in the law shall be judged by the law.
Romans 2:11-12

I saw this kind of behavior go on for years. I was nauseated with the behavior I saw displayed. The pastor was very close to a group of ministers. They had their own clique. No matter what gross sins some of the members committed, they received a slap on the wrist and still functioned in their positions. What I experienced and witnessed was a shame to the entire congregation. This should not be the state of the church.

Dr. Maynard's Panoramic Perspective

Everyone seems to be turning a deaf ear, a blinded eye, and a tied tongue to sin—even those who sit in leadership positions for fear of losing their positions or having an empty church with less tithes and offerings. There was a time when the pastor of the church would address the leader found in error and have them sit down from leadership. People are too arrogant and prideful now to sit down. They would rather go somewhere else than accept they have sinned and must be dealt with. Church folk have not been exposing the devil. They are in a deep slumber, and the devil has taken the land.

The horrible things being exposed about the church are not new. The members who attend the congregation know long before media exposure. The media has a field day at the church's expense. Many people in the congregation and leaders alike turn their heads because they feel it is not their problem to address. On the other hand, they gossip about it. They will not speak of the evil they see to the proper channels to resolve and restore; however, they will speak to defame and let some know that brother or sister "so-so" is on the down low. This is the grave state of church folk's thinking. Now let's look from their side of the tracks. You can tell leadership what you see and they will exclude the person who told them of the evil. It is sad but true. Many times the leaders are in cahoots with the evil being perpetrated. How do we fix this level of distrust amongst church folk?

There are many people in the body of Christ that need solid Christian counseling. The problem is many who have entrusted their secrets have heard what they disclosed in confidentiality discussed throughout the congregation. Many have to move to other churches because of the embarrassment they were caused. This is the grave state of church folk thinking. Many pastors keep their mouths shut because this makes for cheerful givers. The Lord and the pastor love a cheerful giver. I can see the three wise monkeys sitting in a row. The first has his eyes covered. He is blind and gives no direction because he deliberately chooses not to see. If he would simply remove his hands, he would see all that is before him and give some direction. The second monkey covers his ears; he cannot hear by choice. He deliberately blocks out the alarm when it gives warning. He turns a deaf ear to saving souls; he has no faith in what he professes because faith comes by hearing and hearing by the word of God. The third little monkey sits with his mouth covered. He is mute by choice; he refuses to speak the unadulterated truth concerning the word of God. In his mouth lies the power to speak boldly and lead people into the narrow paths. Instead he leads people astray by his silence. Church folk that follow the pattern of the three monkeys will not go unscathed.

 Dr. Lundy's Perspective View

"All scripture is given by inspiration of God, and profitable for doctrine, for reproof, for correction, for instruction in righteousness"
2 Timothy 3:16

Training and development is necessary. People have to be taught that which pertains to God and holiness. People must be teachable and willing to adhere to sound doctrine. I am not talking about a bunch of rules and regulations that change with every whim. I am not talking about outdated traditions designed to keep the church from growing. I am talking about creating an atmosphere to help the church get to the next level, helping people walk in their destiny and reach their potential by applying their God-given gifts and talents.

The church must be in order at all times. The service or program may be formal or informal. There has to be respect across the board, from the oldest to the youngest, from the leaders to the laymen. Humility is necessary to operate on the level God has called you to. Saints must have balance in order to stay grounded. The ability to adjust accordingly and receive constructive criticism is important for great leaders and followers. When a person refuses to follow the guidelines of the church organization it is possible that they are in the wrong church. That does not mean that something is wrong with that person or that church; it just may not be a good fit. If the parties involved cannot come to an understanding—which does not take away from integrity or standards of holiness—decisions must be made to sit the person down until an agreement can be reached.

If a person is sat down, depending on the situation, they should be counseled and restored at the appropriate time if and when the necessary changes have taken place. Sitting a person down is a serious matter and should not be taken lightly by anyone involved. This issue could be devastating to all individuals. As leaders, when we are aware of inappropriate behavior of any kind, it must be addressed. Of course, it is not easy and must be approached with compassion. There should be no double standards. Double standards lead to confusion, dissension, and bad feelings. If you feel that your actions may cause others to go astray, be sensitive to the spirit's leading. We cannot put our heads in the sand and pretend we don't see or hear anything. Do not be afraid that people will leave if they can't have their way. You will not be respected if you just let the devil have his way. The devil will use anybody to take you down, and that person may not even know they are being used. We must watch as well as pray. If you keep giving in to things that you know are wrong, people will leave anyway. We must be the example we are looking for.

Unity in the Church is important in order for the church to run efficiently. I believe God places the pastor and the congregation together. It should be okay to express your opinion in a decent and orderly manner to leadership. No auxiliary or ministry in the church should try to usurp the authority of the pastor. Every pastor is not right for every person. Great prayer is needed for guidance when looking for a church home. Pastors likewise must pray for their placement. If you are not comfortable in a church, and God directs you to leave, you should leave. Just make sure it is the leading of the Lord and not your ego or position-seeking. You will not be blessed unless God is directing you.

-Chapter Sixteen-

HALFWAY SAVED

 Evg. Davis's Reflective Perspective

Over the years I have noticed the moral decline in Christendom. In some places I have visited, I felt like an alien or an outsider. In these current times, what I have become accustomed to as a Christian lifestyle has changed. Today's Christian would say, "It doesn't take all of that." I would probably be ridiculed as being spiritually over the top. These are very different times indeed. Ministers no longer fully believe in what they are teaching others. I knew of a pastor, one I had looked to for spiritual advice and who had been honored for his forty years in service. Having a discussion with him one day, I was shockingly astounded when he said he did not believe all of the scripture and that miracles don't happen today. How can we teach with power if we do not believe what we teach?

There was a time that church folk feared taking communion with unconfessed sin. We don't even give that a second thought nowadays. We casually think about God, his mercy, and long-suffering.

The church is living in a lukewarm state. Dire consequences are coming down the pipe. The church has to go back to the old-time way. The church needs a good old revival. It has to be all or nothing. There is no in between, "no straddling the fence," as the old folk used to say. God is waiting on us. Please, make the change.

For whom the Lord loveth he chasteneth, and scourgeth every son whom he receiveth.
Hebrews 12:6

 Dr. Maynard's Panoramic Perspective

Today, the term "Christian" is used so loosely. You can make your mouth say anything, but where is your heart?

Do not conform to the pattern of this world, but be transformed by the renewing of your mind. Then you will be able to test and approve what God's will is his good, pleasing and perfect will.
Romans 12:2 (NIV)

When we confess with our mouth and believe with our heart that Christ was raised from the dead, that is the beginning but not the end. We have to read the scriptures and come to an understanding of how we should live this Christian life. It is not life on our terms, but what has been written in the word of God for us to live productively. Church folk have to come to a clear understanding that there is no living in the middle of the road. The world offers a life of luxury and pleasures. God can and does provide wealth and pleasures, but of the kind that is healthy to our souls.

No servant can serve two masters: for either he will hate the one, and love the other; or else he will hold to the one, and despise the other. You cannot serve God

and mammon.
Luke 16:13

Church folk cannot live halfway saved. There are now many Christian dating websites and Christian clubs. Fornication should not be a part of getting together. Many people that you will encounter on websites and at clubs are preying on the innocent. These are the "Christians" who can make their mouths say anything. Do not place yourself in bad situations. I was recently viewing a program, and a deacon and a member of the church were dating and having intimate relations. They were talking about it with great calmness on national television without any sense of error or shame. They believed they were not doing anything that was wrong. The church has to educate our young people of the seriousness of fornication.

There is an abundance of topics that could be discussed, too many to fit in this one chapter. There are church folk divorcing at an alarming rate, using drugs, partaking in witchcraft, and the list goes on. It is true that every now and again we may stumble and fall. We must get back up again. We have to examine ourselves and be honest with the results. Make changes where necessary. Christ is returning—will you be ready?

And then shall they see the Son of man coming in a cloud with power and great glory. And when these things begin to come to pass, then look up, and lift up your heads; for your redemption draweth nigh.
Luke 21:27-28

 Dr. Lundy's Perspective View

Therefore if any man be in Christ, he is a new creature: old things are passed away; behold, all things are become new.
2 Corinthians 5:17

When we receive Jesus Christ as our personal savior, we immediately begin a new life. We may not feel or see the manifestation of that transformation right away, but it has started. Now, we must grow.

But grow in grace, and in the knowledge of our Lord and Savior Jesus Christ. To Him be glory both now and forever. Amen.
2 Peter 3:18

Healthy babies are born complete, having everything they need to survive outside of the womb. If they fail to grow normally, something is wrong. When there is a problem, early detection is important. New Christians are like babies, and we that are seasoned need to remember to treat them as such. If they are only preached to, they are not getting the essence of the scriptures. They should be encouraged to study the word both individually and in groups. Sunday school, bible school, and midweek services should be attended where questions can be asked to ensure clarity of scripture. Sunday morning is not the place to get in-depth teaching. A person cannot get what is needed for growth by attending only Sunday morning service. As the concept of salvation is broken down into bite-size pieces, it becomes more digestible and easy to understand. There are those that want to be saved only in church and live a life of sin at other times. Either you are saved or not. There is no middle of the road. Once we get an understanding of the word, we will grow. We will not flip flop back and forth because the word keeps us and we are able to live a life that is no longer ruled by sin.

As newborn babes, desire the sincere milk of the word that ye may grow thereby.
1 Peter 2:2

POETIC NUGGETS FOR THE SOUL

 Evg. Wilcox's Poetic Perspective

Disorder—The New Fabric

Get off that fence; yes, you have a choice.
To listen or reject the Lord's voice.
He may speak with a soft whisper during your busy day.
He's trying to get your attention; allow him to have his way?
I do not know what got you off track.
But the Lord is whispering he wants you back.
So let go of all your fear.
Get alone with the Lord so that you can hear.
For you are unstable like boiling water.
Yes, you are living in total disorder.

Teach and Preach Jesus

Preach Christ at all costs
Your mission is to bring the Gospel to those who are lost.
Hold fast to Christ having your anchor sure and steady.
Make sure when he returns that you are ready.
For without the Lord what would you do to cope?
For without him one is most miserable and without hope.
Live your life with all surety.
For with Christ you have definite security.
Make sure you go into the entire world and preach Christ's name.
Do it with all boldness and without shame.
So that in that final hour you can stand before him without blame.

The Hand of the Diligent

The hand of the diligent soul he will not deny.
The longing of their soul he shall satisfy.
The diligent do not dwell on the past,
But remain unmovable and steadfast.
For they all know only what you do for Christ will last.
Do not look back put your hand to the plow
Yielding to temptation you must not allow.
For Jesus promises to be with you even until the end.
If you get weary do not give up but know you can begin again
For the race is not given to the one that can run real fast
But to the one who can endure and last.

Stinking Thinking

Change your mind; it is the time to hearken unto Gods voice.
It's up to you to make the right choice.
What you need is a tender heart ready to do the Lord's will.
A heart that is pliable, patient and still.
For a deceptive heart is one that is at unrest,
And it keeps God from giving you his best.
So you must let go of anything that holds you back.
Look to Jesus and he will put you on the right track.
For you can have the mind of Christ, oh yes you can.
Think on lovely things and you can stand.
You see a mind that dwells on negative stuff
Is a life that will be hard and rough.
You have to get your head in the game.
When you're in battle don't forget to call Jesus; that's his name.

See, Hear, and Speak No Evil

For the Lord chooses the foolish things to confound the wise.
Nothing takes the Lord by surprise.
Right there in church they fight over a seat.
I even heard some folks lie and cheat.
Not in the house of the Lord for this is forbidden.
For in his word he declares for it is written.
Thou shalt love thy neighbor as thou has loved us.
For it is you that we are supposed to trust.
We must not stay stuck in tradition for this is not the way.
For this is the twenty-first century; it does not work today.
All the gifts work effectively by love.
This is Jesus' word, signed, sealed and delivered from above.

Halfway Saved

Make your calling and election sure.
He has given you strength and you can endure.
He desires a complete surrender; that is what it's all about.
Yes, he wants you to make up your mind to be totally sold out.
There is no almost saved with Jesus.
For he does everything right.
For he is the way.
The truth and the light.
Anyone can be truly saved if they are willing to surrender
Give him your heart; he is the comforter and a heart-mender
He can mend that broken heart.
He'll give you a brand new start.
So make your calling and election sure
He will give you the strength to endure.

-About the Authors-

A. Davis is a servant after God's own heart. This chosen vessel operates under a powerful prophetic and evangelistic anointing. Called to equip the body of Christ with wisdom, knowledge, and instruction, A. Davis resides in Cleveland, OH.

Drs. D.J. Lundy and spouse C.T. Lundy are founders and pastors of the New Dimension Christian Center, located in Staten Island, NY. Dr. Lundy is the author of the book *View from My Window*. In addition, Dr. Lundy is the dean of the Religious Training Institute and Livingston School located in Staten Island, NY. This dynamic preacher is transcending cultural and denominational boundaries and is a sought-after conference speaker.

Dr. M. Maynard is a yielded vessel fueled by the Holy Spirit for service. Dr. Maynard is the author of *Pores Deep: Exuding a Pleasant Fragrance or a Malodorous Stench*. This charismatic preacher and teacher is a sought-after seminar and conference speaker that's proclaiming the empowering message of hope through salvation in Jesus Christ.

C. Wilcox accepted Christ as a young adult and operates in the realm of the prophetic. Since childhood, poetry has always been a great passion. C. Wilcox holds a bachelor's degree in criminal justice and is currently working on a master's in CRJ with a minor in business administration. This poet attributes success to the Almighty God and the continuous support of family.

Truth Serum Publications

Pores Deep
Exuding a Pleasant Fragrance or a Malodorous Stench
By M. Maynard, Ph.D.

The human sense of smell is so powerful that it is able to generate memories and emotions and connect us to our surroundings. We are naturally drawn to pleasant fragrances. At birth, infants develop a sense of their mother's smell; the scent of a cake wafting through the air triggers excitement; and a malodorous stench is universally repulsive! A Christian should have a distinctive aroma that is able to change any atmosphere aromatically.

Allow the unique approach and truths in this book to penetrate your heart. It shares scriptural and fresh revelation on the importance of building a relationship with God and having a servant's heart. "For we are to God the aroma of Christ among those who are being saved and those who are perishing" (2 Corinthians 2:15). Aspire to live a life that exudes a sweet and pleasant fragrance in the nostrils of both God and man.

ISBN # 978-0-9839280-0-3

Truth Serum Publications

View from My Window
By Delores J. Lundy, Ph.D.

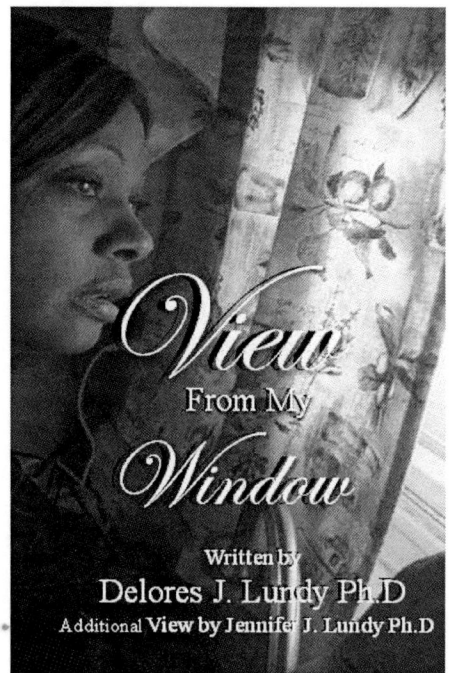

The eyes are the windows of the soul. What you see has a profound effect on you, positively or negatively. Your perception of what you see influences your response. Knowledge or lack of knowledge of the subject matter causes different opinions. Upbringing, exposure, ethnicity, geographic location, education, circles of friends, etc., can influence our response to what we see. We could go on and on about differences, but you only give a view from your window.

ISBN # 978-0-9854436-0-3

Truth Serum Publications

Cobblestone Heart
Lord, Give Me a Heart of Flesh
By M. Maynard, Ph.D.

Coming 2013

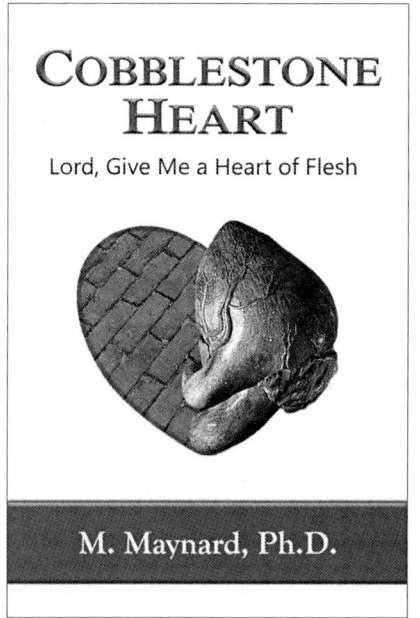

Life's circumstances can sometimes cause hurt and pain, which creates a pavement of stone on the surface of our heart. If we do not guard the heart, we can become hateful, resentful, and even afraid to love. As humans, we sometimes allow challenges to cause us to murmur and complain. We can even find ourselves unable to forgive those who have inflicted wounds, criticism, and rejection.

To be able to walk into the things God has for us and to live life more abundantly, we must have a heart that has been restored. Only a loving God can mold and soften any heart. Simply surrender all and ask, "Lord, give me a heart of flesh."

ISBN # 978-0-9839280-2-7

Truth Serum Publications

Check Your Own Self Out
By Delores J. Lundy, Ph.D.

Coming 2013

When everything around you seems to be turning upside down, it's time to stop and pray and CHECK YOUR OWN SELF OUT.

ISBN # 978-0-9854436-1-0